Loving & Leaving

by Jack Lucci

© Copyright 2023 Jack Lucci

ISBN 978-1-64663-912-0

This is a work of fiction.
All the characters in this book are fictitious,
and any resemblance to actual persons, living or dead,
is purely coincidental. The names, incidents, dialogue,
and opinions expressed are products
of the author's imagination and
are not to be construed as real.

Published by

 köehlerbooks™

3705 Shore Drive
Virginia Beach, VA 23455
800-435-4811
www.koehlerbooks.com

Loving & Leaving

JACK LUCCI

VIRGINIA BEACH
CAPE CHARLES

Table of Contents

I was running out of space
to keep my memories.

OLIVE

The Merchants was a large restaurant with an indoor balcony running along the roofline. Along the balcony, there was enough space for a table with two chairs and a waiter to deliver orders. The tables were buttoned up against a brick wall, and the lighting below was ambient, leaving a soft light for the balcony above. Diners could overlook the kitchen, where they could observe the operations from a bird's-eye view. There was never a shortage of "corner" spoken loudly by the staff to alert others around blind corners. The Merchants was a counter service restaurant, where orders were taken by a cashier, and a numbered placard, corresponding to the order number, was placed on the table. The table markers were playing cards, and when I was a kid, I always hoped for an ace of spades. The Merchants shut down for a few years, and another restaurant rented the space. Olive was essentially the same, Mediterranean, or at least tried to be. I applied for a position as I became increasingly aware that a gig in the restaurant industry would fit me properly. Somewhat of a wild animal, I rarely stayed inside my cage.

I was living as I would continue to live for many years. I shared an apartment with a friend, Marco. We drank and smoked more nights than we didn't, as we were slowly coming into our own. We both held gigs at rather prominent eateries downtown, and in southeastern Washington, wine flows like water; one can expect to be paid in it. Marco is someone I think I'd kill for. Many can recall a time when life was ordinary, easy to navigate, and yet, still, just over the horizon, problems existed and fit a frame that slowly expanded. The easiest part of living is *to* live; accepting it is another thing. Marco and I were in our early twenties, with a true love for each other. We had met at some age, somewhere, and no matter the particulars, we were brothers. We used to fight and bicker like children, but, after all, we were. When I was too drunk to stand, Marco held me up by my armpits while I pissed in the grass. Once, I watched him fall down a flight of stairs and pop up like he meant to do it. We had a pet, an iguana; we took care of the little bastard, but he hated us. We named him Lizard Man, and he's probably dead by now. We gave Lizard Man to some reptile freak we found on Craigslist, but I didn't trust him. Marco was my most encouraging drinking partner, my voice of drunken blunder. Marco's parents brought him here from Mexico when he was one year old, and I'm glad they did. He claimed he could drink a bottle of El Jimador and not be hungover the next morning, and most of the time, he wasn't. I love Mexican culture, especially the women. The food and booze are world-class, and they are all fantastic dancers.

There is something about choosing one's family, being

accepted while simultaneously accepting in the process. One of the more surprising aspects of growing up is knowing love for a man and love for a woman. Both sexes are vastly different, and each require a different set of necessities. I can't imagine I am any good with women, as I tend to keep a brotherly sort of love toward them. I forget to buy them gifts or fail to read them well long-term. Apparently, I am terrible at reading what a woman wants. For the first few weeks after meeting, I can predict them successfully, but by the time the excitement is over, I begin to trail off—an awfully disastrous nature that never seems to end well.

I met Kat on my first day at Olive. I was immediately taken. I hadn't laid eyes on such a specimen. I knew I had to have her. It was a jolt, all at once—I knew it. She either felt it too, or she would come to feel that same emotion eventually. A month in, I had her. Kat was gentle and held few judgments. She was easily swayed by those around her and seemed yet to know exactly who she was. Not an uncommon trait, it seems to be quite prevalent among those more docile. Something about her twisted me; I needed to know her. She was slowly finding herself, and I enjoyed discovering it with her. Kat was in the tail end of a long-term relationship before we met, and I think she was more needy than she was prepared to reenter the dating world. Like most things in life, it all comes down to timing, and unfortunately, I am far from punctual. Kat and I shared nights in my apartment, staring out the French windows, talking, and lying naked in the shadows cast by lamplight. She kissed me like she wanted to be guided, like she wanted to be told what to do. Eventually, she began to bore me; I lost interest. Such is my inclination that I began to take her for granted like she was a work buddy who I fucked sometimes.

When I was a kid, my parents took me to Las Vegas, and my father showed me the pit where he worked as a craps dealer in the 1980s. The buildup of going to a new place had me excited, and when we arrived, it was breathtaking. My eyes shot open at all the lights and the pornography littered in the streets, the smell of cigarettes in the casinos, and the life my dad once lived. After a day, I became bored and wanted to leave. Interested in the flash no longer, I stared over the strip from Excalibur, longing to see New York City.

Weeks after I began working at Olive, I was introduced to a new hire, Claire. I was tasked with showing her the ropes and the duties pertaining to a shift. I was to show her the gears that grind. Claire was petite with large eyes. Her eyes were disproportionate to her delicate frame, yet they somehow fit perfectly on her face. Claire attended Whitman College and was studying psychology or maybe sociology—I can't quite remember. She was sharp as a blade and shined like stainless steel. Hailing from Northern California, she had a sunny disposition. She wore a mischievous grin that seldom left her face. Her hair was light brown, her eyes matching in hue.

We got along fine. I felt comfortable with her. She was popular among her peers, as she wore her heart on her sleeve. We discovered that we lived in the same building; I was on the third floor, and she was on the fifth. Slowly but steadily, we became good friends. I began to confide in her. She never appeared bored or discontent. It was as if she knew, under the surface, there was a person she longed to see. She was willing to hear me and remained open to listening, always. I still feel as though she cares about me, even after all this time. She extended herself to my never-ending turbulence, the unceasing inconsistency. I was open with her and felt a real connection.

I never lied to Claire, as I would hate to betray her. We were a team no matter how far apart our hearts may have been. Claire was dating a guy from Whitman, and I only hoped he was good to her. I was chasing Kat who already had a home. She went back to her ex as so many others do. I didn't mind much since I had an out. Claire shared everything about herself and spoke unencumbered. I could listen to her for hours; the sound of her voice was my favorite song. I could tell by her smile that she was happy, and that, in turn, made me happy. I love Claire's smile—pure and free of malice. I used to put on a sort of performance, an informal song and dance. I only wanted to see a smile spread across her face.

I made some other friends and connections. I met those who party, and by party, I mean partake. Cocaine is like a centipede. Once on it, one has one hundred legs. Feel it crawl inside your face. Feel it drip down toward your belly. There is a certain camaraderie that connects drug users. It has something to do with shared desires or goals. I had a partner in crime, Jon. He liked painkillers more than I did, and that surprised me. He carried a flapped baggie; the color of its contents resembled a rainbow, all guaranteed to lay you out. I would throw him some cash, and he would pull out a few pills, all varying in size and color, hand them over to me, and pop a couple himself— for good measure. Jon didn't last long at Olive. He got caught stealing from the cash register, pocketing about six grand. He stole a $100 bill from the register every day for about two months, until he was eventually caught and subsequently fired. Jon had an aggressive addiction that demanded hundreds of dollars every day. Eventually, he went to rehab and was reduced to living on the street after his first relapse. I'm not sure how he got away with it for so long, but if an addict is anything, he is surely shifty.

I used one of the three public bathrooms Olive provided. Each one was a single-person bathroom and had a lock. I put the green pill, diamond shaped, in between a folded dollar bill and laid a credit card on top. Pushing down, with force, I carefully created the crumble. I unfolded the dollar and neatly dumped the powder out. Using the credit card to cut the pile into thirds, I performed the surgery unfailingly. I disassembled a BIC Cristal pen, discarding the ink cartridge, tip, and back plunger. Using scissors, I cut the hollowed pen, trimming off about a quarter. I railed a line, took a piss, railed a line, washed my hands, railed a line, and out the door. I was smacked in sixty seconds. I thought the daytime demanded it, as I worked better when high.

I met Brandon my first day at Olive. A Black dude with rhythm, he loved to sing and didn't sound half bad. An honestly warm person, he was friendly with everyone he met. We worked late nights together, getting high in the basement, having heart-to-hearts. He especially loved wine; we drank cases in our day. He was in a constant state of party. Cocaine and wine mixed with good people. He came alive by nightfall. The sun shuttered to rise as our early mornings were spent tableside, cutting, chopping, snorting, and blasting.

By this time, I was smacking pills in the sunshine and railing blow by moonlight. I was spiraling; I was having fun, but I was spiraling, nonetheless. I told Claire what I was doing. She hated it but never showed anger. We would sit on the bricks in the back, smoke cigarettes, and talk. Staring over empty parking spaces, breathing in the night, we existed together. When I had moments of a sober mind, they were almost always spent with her.

It was slowly at first, then I suddenly realized I had to get out of the situation I created for myself. I was becoming dependent and needed a drastic change of scenery as southeastern Washington was beginning to fit too tight. I wanted to see the world, and there was little to stop me. Claire came over before I left for the airport. We sat on the couch with only empty boxes as furniture. Marco was moving in with in his girlfriend, Lyds, whom he eventually married. Their love grew like thick ivy, hard to remove and invasive. I was their ornery love child, trying desperately to cause a stir. Lyds never wavered, and she began to grow on me. Marco had Lyds now, and I was happy for him. I really couldn't have convinced him of anyone better, as I failed to ever find one. I handed him to her; the humor in that is that I needed him more than he needed me. Over the prior few days, they began their move and were almost finished.

Claire's shoulder was resting against mine. Counteracting the force against them, Claire kept me up most days. She had her own life, and I loved being a part of it. It pains me now as I sit and think of how I should have been a much larger part.

"It's wild how fast a year goes. It seems like yesterday you were showing me how to polish a wine glass," she said, smiling wide and turning to me.

"Like most things in my life, I assumed this trip would never come. I've been a real mess the past few months. We could have been something, something real, you know?"

"You think so? I do too. The timing never worked," said

Claire "I was with Sam there for a while, and you were, well, like you said . . .."

She sat back, both of us smiling—smiling like kids. I looked around the room and back at her. I noticed a tear collecting on her eyelid, almost spilling over, and when our eyes met, it did. A single tear streamed down her face, yet she wore a smile so bright, so pleasantly placed amidst the sadness in her eyes. In that moment, I hated to see the tear, thinking I caused it, and for everything she gave me, all I could offer her was to put that smile there. She was deeply and highly intelligent, collected, confident, silly, and off the cuff. She was funny and perfectly dastardly in jest. She appeared to be cut from glass, as her frame was delicate with sharp edges. Claire is beautiful in the classical sense, eternally striking and earnestly genuine. She never lied, and she had this way of divulging naked truths. I leaned on her for the things that troubled me. She was next to me, smiling as she does in that oversized Whitman sweater, which served as more of a dress. She was a person to spend time with, as no moment was ever dull with her. She brings life with her wherever she goes.

I kissed her before the tear fell from her chin, pressing it against my face, trying to dry her eyes with mine. Like a calm before the storm, our lips moved slowly, then faster as I began to take her in. I moved her to my lap, placing my arms around her back. I wanted her more than I wanted to explore. All at once, I knew it was dangerous. Her breaths were heavy, and I could feel her heart pumping. I kissed her neck to give her air, and she came up to breathe only to come down again. There was something in that moment. I can recall it so clearly, like staring through glass. I loved Claire, and even though I hadn't realized it until that moment, I knew it was true. We resumed the position longer, tasting each other.

"I'm going to write to you every day. It might take some time for the letters to get to you, but they'll come."

She whispered, "I love you. I'll look for them every day."

I kissed her harder, gratefully regretful.

IN FARA SABINA

Italy seemed appropriate. I had never been anywhere east of Pittsburgh. Coming from a small town, I found the world to be especially grandiose, too large to ever cover completely, so I thought I'd start with Italy. I watched this movie three months prior where the main character travels there, becomes infatuated with a young woman, and falls in love. Eventually, she is found to be a vampire, but our main character doesn't seem to mind. Up until a point in my life, a most recent point, I think I only ever wanted to fall in love. I always liked the idea of having a person that, in a way, made me whole.

I landed on Italy for the simple reason that I am Italian. It was somewhat shallow and predictable but a logical choice at that. The Colosseum or the statue of *David* are just obscure relics history had long discovered. I assumed the sun shined the same, and the moon still moved the tides. I didn't know what to expect as I planned the trip with a messy hand in a hurried pace.

I felt it was imperative to speak the tongue. I enrolled in a language school in Florence for the first month. The Istituto Il David is a school where the focus is to teach the language and the customs of Italian culture. Through the David school, I was able to secure a month of housing on the third floor of a large building in a block of flats on a street who's name I couldn't pronounce. I planned for the trip to last roughly three months, and though money would be tight, I was determined to make it work. I sold my car to travel there, a decision I do not regret. I planned the trip in early February, departed early April, returned in a young July, and left in late August. It was a year, a year spent swimming.

The time came fast, and I left my life behind. Plans that started blurrily were suddenly manifest. I found myself at the airport clutching a single bag, having yet to fully realize that, for three months, I was leaving the confines of the only country and culture I'd ever known. Maybe I was too wide-eyed to fully conceptualize the gravity, but I was burning to get out. I boarded a plane from Seattle to Toronto, then Toronto to Munich, and finally, Munich to Florence. It was a hellish travel day, one where I lost hours of sleep and most of my sanity as the jet lag set in. The airport in Munich had these little rooms where one can chain-smoke cigarettes. My lungs saturated with smoke, I sat in the enclave, running on no sleep, lighting smoke after smoke, taking drag after drag. A little while later, I meandered to a bar. Not much had changed between Munich and southeastern Washington.

Four beers in Munich, and I'd say I was ready to leave.

Sitting there, taken, chatting with a German woman of maybe thirty years, the bartender, she had soft eyes and a beaming smile. A man sat to my left, more drunk than I was. Judging by his accent, he was Polish, but then again, Eastern Europeans tend to borrow from each other. He was vile and spoke in broken English; his two favorite words were "fuck" and "pussy," as he said them frequently. Leaning over to me, smelling of vodka, he shared his sexual fantasies concerning our German friend. I nodded, smiling. I could not disagree with his desires, as I, too, shared a few. The German was tall for a woman, at least for a woman in the States. Soft features with piercing blue eyes. A blue like the oceans I crossed to get here, a blue like the sky I flew under. Blond like the wheat fields of my hometown in early summer. I wondered what she was doing in this airport. She had the qualifications of a model, and I thought maybe all German women were as attractive as her.

I knew a German girl once, Clara. A stunningly beautiful blond with legs like stilts, skin smooth like satin, and eyes one could fall into. Her laugh was her most attractive attribute, and she loved to smile. Year's prior, she dated one of my roommates, Karl. She was the type of person one knew was going somewhere; it was just a matter of time before she got there. A world traveler, she knew three languages and projected a sense of confidence. Fear appeared to be entirely absent from her life.

After all these years, I can still see her in that baby-blue silk dress that hung mid-thigh. The dress fit her perfectly; it looked like it was made to be worn on her body. She experimented with hair color and often made drastic cuts to the length and style. After she dumped Karl and he moved out, she would come over, and we would sit on my couch, talking until the wine took over and we could no longer sit idle. Holding her set me right with the world. She fit like a puzzle piece in my arms, curving into me naturally, talking of travel plans in between French kisses. We connected mentally; we seemed to share a common thirst for knowledge and enjoyed picking apart the imperfect philosophies of thinkers we admired. I found that fucking took a back seat for the first time in my life. I was pleased to part ways at the end of the night, walking her to her car, telling jokes, and kissing her goodbye. I remember watching her taillights trail down Boyer Avenue, hoping it wasn't the last time I saw her. Eventually, it was, as she moved to somewhere in Europe. Somewhere, she was splitting a bottle of wine with a guy who talks in a funny accent, but I liked to think of her as happy, and the thought of her satin skin glistening under a European sun made me happy.

Finally, I boarded. Finally, I was on the last leg of my journey. After one more miserable hour hurling through the air by way of a small plane, I'd ultimately meet my destination. Upon descending, the pilot flew the tube over the rolling hills of Tuscany—a sight for sore eyes as I felt a pull toward the earth. I felt the landing gear open, and when the wheels hit the runway, I knew I was home.

I deplaned, then hailed a taxi. I spoke English, whereas the driver may as well have been deaf. I showed him the address I had written down an hour before, consisting of some numbers in the San Jacopino neighborhood. He smiled. Obviously, he knew the place. Sitting in the back of that cab, I struggled to stay awake. I fixed my gaze on the surrounding architecture, which, to me, looked alien. Apartment structures and modern homes make tourists uninterested. But I found the observation of the ordinary to be the most astounding. What struck me was the construction of these homes. Relative to the life I put on hold, this was another planet. Perfect squares and cut lines, almost all with rooftop patios. Street signs in foreign languages, and the smell in the back of this cab. I suddenly realized the shift; I realized the transfer. I was a house plant in new soil, a simple clump of roots surrounded by new dirt and housed in a brand-new pot.

We arrived at 1900 hours. I had never seen the number nineteen on a clock before. It took me a while to adjust. I met my host on the curb, and she ushered me up quickly. She tore through her assortment of keys until she decided on one that looked ancient. She inserted the key, and the towering door slowly swung open. Her name was Angelina, and she was as old as the building itself. She only spoke Italian and still insisted on verbal communication. She showed me around the apartment, taking a left from the door to the bedrooms and bathroom in the back. Going to the right, I passed through the kitchen, feeding into the dining room, housing a small rectangular table with a bright yellow tablecloth, four chairs, and a small television. Past the dining room was the last bedroom, where I would sleep for the duration. There were two twin-size beds, maybe six feet apart. They sat underneath a casement window overlooking the back courtyard and the restaurant below. The email I received stated I should expect roommates, as they would also be my classmates. I was the only tenant in the entire apartment my whole stay in Florence, and I quite liked the privacy. I only ever had one guest.

Angelina then moved me back to the dining room, where we

drank red wine from a bottle with no label, and she blathered on for twenty minutes in Italian, of which nothing was understood. Eventually, she left me with the keys, continuing in Italian and with no regard for my lack of comprehension. I proceeded to the bedroom and forced the two twin beds together, hoping to create more space, but as soon as I plopped down, I had not noticed a difference; I was out like a light. I gave the first night to rest in Florence, a deal I was willing to make. If I had anything there, it was surely an abundance of time.

The next morning, I walked out of the apartment, and as soon as my foot hit the pavement, I felt Florence inside of me. A numinous experience, one I won't soon forget. Crossing Viale Rosselli onto Alamanni and Luigi, I stumbled into Piazza Della Stazione. It is an open space, a courtyard of sorts, and home to many patio restaurants and trattorias, gelato shops, and pharmacies. I needed to eat, as my stomach was bellowing, and I noticed my thirst increasing. I wanted fine wine and pasta, maybe even a woman. I hadn't decided yet, but I knew that hunger would eventually call. I landed on some restaurant whose name I couldn't pronounce. I ordered a plate of amatriciana and a bottle of Sangiovese. The day was young, early afternoon, and I could feel a spirit seeking me. A spirit some have felt—a spirit of hope and the cool rush of wind when riding a bike downhill. I found something in Florence, and something found me.

The next day was day one of the thirty-day intensive language course at the David school. In hindsight, I should have known my commitment to attend would waver only a week in the program. Firenze worked a bustle inside my chest, spun my head at every corner, and replaced any desire to study.

The streets were uneven, but I traversed them intently. Most days were spent drinking espresso or grappa from a small shot glass, eating pizza on the steps of the Duomo, and acting as photographer for many tourists, both foreign and domestic. I wanted to live inside the streets. I wanted to enter them and become one with the concrete.

The sun is blinding when seen straight on. Florence's sun lit a sky far brighter than the heavens, bathing in the light her bones borne and outstretched. I wandered in a dress shirt, three top buttons unbuttoned, shades to shield my eyes, and a cigarette dancing between my lips. I wrote to Claire every day in Florence. A welcomed anchor, I enjoyed the thought of returning to her and explaining my sojourn in greater detail. I mostly wrote at night, smoking cigarettes and drinking Birra Moretti. I liked to think of the man on the bottle as a friend. We had conversations in my head, but he wasn't much for talking.

My desire for a woman strengthened as I started to flirt with Karina from England who had dark hair and a small build. She was from Manchester, if memory serves. She wore two cheek dimples the size of sinkholes. She was older than me, maybe thirty-two years old, and being an eleutheromaniac, she never made plans. She giggled often and had a funny way of talking.

Karina attended the David school but skipped with me to tear up the streets and run afoul in a foreign land. I loved her accent and the way she sounded when she climaxed. It was like hearing music in a foreign language, a new take on an old classic. Karina was sensual; she loved to drink and fuck. I wondered if she had a man back in England, but our conversations never went there. We talked about what we wanted to do and not what we did.

We smoked cigarettes in bed and shared a thin cotton blanket. The air in Florence was enveloping, and most of the time, it was all she needed, walking the apartment naked. In the early afternoon, after our morning wine, she loved to be naked. She loved her body, and I loved it too. I took her in my mouth; she tasted of Chianti, wet as wine. Karina could have been my wife in another life, but maybe that was just Florence. On our last night, we went to Ponte Vecchio after dark and fucked blatantly on the bridge. She was going to Greece the next day, and I was headed south, still unsure of my destination, but that could be decided later. I walked her to the apartment she rented on Via Della Stuta, where we embraced for the last time. She still has a piece of me if she chose to retain it. Florence, a magnificent city with a more magnificent woman.

I stopped at a bar for a nightcap and ended up too drunk to walk home. I woke up in bed, having no idea how I got there. I remember falling and smacking my shoulder on the pavement, but little is known after that. I was in Florence's hands, and she treated me kindly. Florence was breathing, her chest moving to the beat of footsteps, a steady march, keeping pace. She was a pleasure to know. Her more affable characteristics came through when exploring her structures. There are no shortages of tourists or people just passing through; her bricks have been tested. Florence can handle the attention. She has a special place saved for me inside the shadow of Medici Manor. Roads doubling as walkways, vehicles allowing safe passage, a grand scene for all to see. The beautiful people spend cash amongst the gypsies, who pray to the God of change. I was in my own lane, as I had not enough to shop at Gucci but just enough for wine. The sun washes over Florence, sweeps across Santo

Spirito, until finally glinting down across the Arno. There are overwhelming hues of red in Florence. It may be due to the Duomo, but it was something else, something inherent. The blood of Florence is the people; they carry oxygen through her circulatory system, using streets as her veins.

I said goodbye to her and gave a kiss before parting. I boarded a train and headed southeast for Bari. I find that a single goodbye is sufficient for most departures in life, as both Florence and Karina were in my past now. Bari is on the southeastern coast near the heel of the boot. I love Bari. If Bari was a person, it would be my best friend. I was there for a handful of days; the exact number is a bit of a blur, as I somehow managed to time my stay while a festival was happening. People were in the streets all night long, dancing and drinking, living life without a phone in sight. I existed primarily on seafood and beer and stayed in a filthy hostel. Hostels are something, something not describable, each as unique as the last, housing strange times and stranger people. Many languages fly around the rooms, and there is a persistent odor of sex.

I stayed in Polignano a Mare for a few days to recharge my batteries, and by recharge, I mean time spent on a beach, bottle in hand. I wandered into a restaurant; the window held seals saying, "Michelin rated." At the time, I had no idea what that strange French word meant. I was overlooking the inlet, seated next to a table of wealthy Italians, a man with two attractive women adorned in gold jewelry. L'Osteria di Chichibio is a marvelous place, almost chiseled from the cliffside that holds it. I sat on the deck and stared over the ocean. I watched a single sailboat pass on calm waves. I ordered some sort of risotto and a bottle of wine, enjoying that part of the day.

Later, I stumbled into a quiet bar and drank beer outside, letting the night come. I had several conversations with strangers while smoking cigarettes and slurring my words. I found the way to my apartment and fell into bed. I woke up at 3:30 a.m. with knives tearing at my stomach and twisting my insides. I hadn't purchased water prior to the bender, so I relied on tap water that needed to be boiled before drinking. I stared at the water in the pot. Gruelingly, I watched bubbles begin to collect at the bottom, indicating a slow rise to boil. My body was weak, and my wallet was light. I knew I had to get grounded. I had taken enough time twisting around the countryside drunk and off my ass.

After Polignano, I went all the way south to Calabria to visit where my grandparents lived before immigrating to Pennsylvania. A lively city, it was an attraction for the more ambitious tourist, as more popular locations are seated up north. I traveled to other cities, but like most of my time wandering around Southern Italy, it was somewhat of a blur—a month-long excursion on trains and inside bars, drinking with the locals. When traveling, one should only patronize establishments not marketed to tourists. What a waste to travel and experience a version of life created by corporations to attract the novice traveler. Go, get lost and figure it out.

Today's technology can be quite helpful in terms of locating resources. A sort of Craigslist exists for those looking for work when traveling. I lived on a farm in Fara Sabina on the outskirts of a village called Mompeo. My first family was Yvonne and Giuliano, or Giuli, as Yvonne called him. She was a fat woman and a good partner in wine. For health reasons, Giuli gave up the stuff, but that didn't stop Yvonne and me. From what I could collect after meeting other farmers in the area, my hosts had an affinity for wine and cigarettes. Giuli only spoke Italian, and his English was difficult to understand. Our conversations were short and generally work-related. Yvonne was a fluent English speaker and translated our conversations. I traded labor for shelter and quite possibly the best zuppa di fagioli on planet Earth. Tending to olive trees and performing basic landscaping, I found the work rewarding. It helped to mold a sense of self-reliance in me. I learned how to live in partial isolation, as I became very close to the souls I shared a home with.

I moved light in my journey to Fara Sabina and failed to carry necessities. One thing about rural Italy is that food and water for sale on trains are sparse and often nonexistent. The train rides, totaling thirteen hours, were void of food and water, but there were plenty of cigarettes and mountain views. Some smokers on the train propped a door open to smoke, a courteous action, as there was poor ventilation. I approached a man smoking, bothering him for a light.

Gianni was six foot in boots and had curly hair, almost an afro. He was traveling around like I was and had no care for the destination. Gianni was going to Rome for the day, bright-eyed and smelling of wine. In a foreign language, he spoke of a full-frontal woman and a failed love who was close enough for him to touch, yet when he stretched, she became distant and out of reach. I understood what I could, and I don't envy the man. From the sound of it, he was leaving after love, just like I was. He also cherished cigarettes, and I imagined us being friends in another life.

From Calabria to Napoli to Roma, I went on trains in

between towns and villages with names I fail to recall. I arrived in Fara Sabina's train station and met my hosts for the first time. The woman jumped from the front seat and extended a warm embrace. She forcefully opened the door to her silver Peugeot, and out of sorts, I tumbled in. From the station, their home was an hour away through winding hills and primitive roads, past a decommissioned rock quarry and endless fields of olive trees. I sat in the back seat of their Peugeot, sick from the bends, lips chapped and stomach screaming. Pitch-black like I had never seen before, there was only the light from the speedometer to break through the darkness. We arrived, and I informed them that I had nothing to eat or drink that entire day and felt as if my body was on fire; they rushed me into their home quickly, offering dried meats and Pecorino cheese, wine mixed with water, and everything else in their kitchen. I felt as if I had offended them by my lack of sustenance. Judging by their reaction, I'd think this was a crime to have an empty stomach—something about Italians, full hearts, and even fuller bellies.

Old-school Italian man, Giuli—not like a New Jersey Italian but a real Italian. He spoke with his hands. He was probably six feet, six inches and had size fourteen boots. From the north, he loved bodies of water, and in his younger days, he sailed for a living. Yvonne was Belgian but easily mistaken for one of our own, as she essentially was. If she was not Italian, I do not know anyone who is.

The next day, I suited down for work; rain had moved in, so my first day was cut in half. I didn't mind, as I could use this time to recover. From what little work I did that day, I had a lot to take away. Travel can humble the proudest of men, shedding the comforts of native tongue. Leaving behind accustomed culture forces the foreigner to gain a new perspective, to live outside of digestible tradition, and watch and learn, at first from afar and then up close. One must learn customs in the homes of those who practice them, for there is little to be gained in the way of worldviews through the sole study of books. To experience is to risk, and that is where the individual learns his values and lives according to his own self-interest. What do men value beyond that of satisfaction or the desire to see it done, simply for the fact of doing, for the fact of existing? Yes, the olive trees are pleasing, and the country is calming, but what drives a man toward the tilling of land, and what motivates him to continue? I discovered nothing matters except completing the task.

Giuli and I needed to move gravel from his shed to the lower part of his driveway. We put on gloves and started shoveling rock into a wheelbarrow that appeared to be constructed in the late nineteenth century. Many tools on his farm were primitive, and I believe this was on purpose. Giuli, from what I could gather, was a wealthy man. Up to that point, I had no idea what his career had been, but judging by his property, his home, and pictures of a lake house up north, he was surely well off. After filling the wheelbarrow to the brim, we carefully began to descend the drive. The front wheel was rickety and moved side to side under the weight of the rocks. I lost control, and the wheelbarrow tipped, spilling the contents. We looked at each other, unable to verbally communicate, and for a second, I didn't know what to do. He looked at me square in the eyes, seeing my soul for only a moment; then he looked down at the mess of gravel at our feet and began to pile it back into the wheelbarrow.

It was like being thrown from a moving vehicle straight into a brick wall. It was a moment of extreme clarity and utter revelation. When the contents of life spill out, pick them back up. It's that simple, that obvious, and that resounding. Pick up the fucking contents and move forward. Giuli presumably did not take notice of the profundity he imparted in me, for he was as strong as an ox and most likely born with this mentality. I, however, was not, and it is still a lesson I study. I traveled to Italy to outrun an OxyContin addiction and the inability to cope with the perception of love lost. I was a petulant child and probably still am, but in those days, all I knew to do was run, and that's exactly what I did. I didn't run on that day. I bent over and gathered the gravel back into the wheelbarrow, maneuvering intently to finish the job.

I made mistakes often, and on a day in late spring, Yvonne was in the kitchen, as usual, and Giuli and I were outside landscaping. My translator was not present, so Giuli and I had to rely on sign language, pointing, and primal sounds. I thought I knew what he tasked me with, so I began. When he returned, he was dismayed to see I had begun to cut out a large chunk of grass from his well-kept lawn. Shouts in Italian sound like those in English, yet they strike me to the bone and are much more frightening. Yelling for Yvonne, she approached us mid-translation. I was to cut around the grass to create an edge, not dig up the existing sod.

In the evenings, we watched American television. Yvonne loved *CSI: Miami*. She had great adoration for Mr. Caine, the main character. The sound her voice made whenever The Who started playing was of pure joy, and like a child, her eyes would light up. She would shout, "Mr. Caine! Mr. Caine! Mr. Caine!"

The episodes were dubbed in Italian. I remember thinking that even though it wasn't Mr. Caine's authentic voice, she cared little for the difference. After long days in the field of backbreaking work, I would return to their home, shower, then muster any remaining strength I had to walk downstairs and eat dinner. How gracious they both were, and how grateful I am for it. Yvonne was a pure talent in the kitchen, an absolute master of the wooden spoon, world-class in her skills. She demanded the finest ingredients and prepared meals as if it was her passion to see fullness in others. Giuli was spoiled, to say the least.

I have the impression that cooking was not just her job in the home but her purpose. The shining achievement was to satisfy Giuli and any guests that may have the pleasure of sitting at her table. Veal cutlets, salad from the garden, and dishes I had never seen before. Everything was drenched in oil made from olives, which grew just beyond the back door. Every dish was chased with wine. I liked to mix a half cup of white with a half cup of red; something about mixing the best qualities of both brought the drink to life.

One evening after work, we congregated around the table, same as any other night. On this night, though, I was to expect guests. People from the next farm over, the ones whose wine I imbibed daily and nightly, were coming over to size up Yvonne and Giuli's guest. There was no shortage of work to be done; however, there was a shortage of workers. I was to potentially stay with them for the next month and work to prepare olive trees for the autumn harvest. Apparently, I satisfied them, as I was contracted out. Looking back, I was more of a commodity than I was a man. I was merely a mule to be rented out, put to work, and fed. How I wish to return there now, to be seen for my skill and ethic, to be considered for my ability rather than respected simply because I exist. I worked for everything I received in Fara Sabina. I found that if not for my ability to work, I would have never met these people who I grew so close to.

The rest of my time with Yvonne and Giuli was spent working and chatting, with two bottles of wine over lunch and maybe three over dinner. Yvonne had a golden heart, yet gold, as a comparison, is insufficient. She would take me along on her grocery store journeys and was a delight to spend time with. When outside of the home, I stayed close to her, as I felt as foreign as I was. She would tell me about her time in Belgium as a young girl, where she learned most of her culinary skills, and about how she lost her father at a young age. She was warm like the feeling of tea on a cold day or ten more minutes of bed in the morning. She had a smile that made my heart smile and a laugh to conjure the dead. Yvonne was a mother to me, and I love her like one. They have no children of their own, but I consider myself theirs.

After three weeks, I packed what few possessions I had and migrated to the next farm over. The farmer's name was Katarina, or Katae, and she studied wolves at the University of Rome. She had a husband and a stepdaughter who were both in Rome for the summer. He was doing work, and she was going to school. There was another woman working and living on Katae's farm as a worker and friend; her name was Rebecca, or Rebe. She was from Stockholm and was intent on becoming a full-blooded Italian. She spoke Italian nearly perfectly and loved the culture, the people, the food, and the work. A marginally attractive young woman, close to me in age and with few options for bodily connections, we spent many nights together. Rebe and I stayed in a smaller home up the hill from Katae, a sort of guesthouse or separate quarters. I remember being drunk on homemade wine and fucking her until we passed out naked with the windows open, breathing in the mountain air. Katae never knew of our secret intimacy. I presume she would have cared little about it, but we genuinely enjoyed sneaking around. Rebe was quite adventurous in bed. She loved giving oral sex and equally loved to receive it. There were two rooms in our cabin; we seldom entered the other. We were covered in dirt by day and soaked in sweat by night. I was quite forceful with her, pinning her down and having my way. Judging by her moans, she yearned for passion, and her bodily reactions confirmed my advantage. Falling into each other, we rolled around in bed. Low light from the moon caressed her figure and served as our only light. Our mouths sucking spit and licking sweat off each other's bodies—she tasted like olives and was sweet like a cherry.

Work was more demanding on Katae's farm. She possessed more land than Guili and Yvonne, with hectares of olive trees. The first job I performed was collecting and chopping wood for the winter months. I felt especially useful as I was providing the materials for heating her home in the winter. Katae was nothing special in the kitchen, but what she lacked there, she made up for in spirit. I survived on our conversations, as she has a depth to her. She had a mind for passion and found pleasure in explaining weather systems for this particular part of Italy. She knew the history of the area and would pull over on the highway whenever she thought she saw a wolf. Katae owned an olive oil company that exported to other countries in Europe. From the looks of it, she ran a successful business.

I spent days collecting wood for the winter, walking across her many hectors, and exploring the fields. Every twenty feet or so, there stood an olive tree. The roll of the hills was staggering and turned my legs to jelly more times than once. Often, I got lost, but I always found my way back home. Katae had horses that roamed the property. Rudimentary fences lined the boundaries but still stood strong and served their purpose. I remember once, three or four of them approached my position and sat down next to me. Somewhat nervously, I joined them to sit. Horses are quite calm creatures when they want to be and are kind to humans. While sitting among the horses, I waved the flies out of their eyes; they allowed me to rub my hand across their heads politely. Once they were finished with their break, they immediately stood up to part, stunning in size. Witnessing a horse stand to rise while sitting next to it is a formidable sight, as their size is overwhelming, pure strength with forceful movement. I had to quickly alter my position so as not to be crushed.

After all the wood was gathered and stored, I moved on to collecting hay for those same horses. I amassed large piles, ten feet high and ten feet wide. It was to be left to dry, then bailed and kept upstairs in the barn. This was a grueling process, and I worked for every meal. Chickens and goats also lived on the property, and in conjunction with Fulmony, the dog, we ran a tight ship. Occasionally, the male goat would decide to leave and go in search of other females, as if his seven weren't enough. Fulmony would chase him and attempt to corral him back, but if unsuccessful, the goat would turn up days later, looking for his nannies. Goats are most interesting creatures, not exactly to my taste or liking. I ate goat stew there, and while grateful for the meal, it was not my favorite. Goats are portrayed and likened to the devil in the Bible. I imagine it is due to their sense of free will, as this male goat certainly had his.

Mompeo is an ancient city built on a hill. While wandering the cobblestones, I liked to think of the stories of the townspeople, their comings and goings, and their obviously close relationships. Katae, Rebe, and I once wandered upon a six-hundred-year-old bocce ball court that was entirely still in use. The gambling and drinking that must have taken place there was really something to ponder. There was a single general store in Mompeo, a pharmacy of sorts but little in the way of medicine. Stale chips and cookies were rarely purchased, as people had little use for the processed garbage that is so prevalent in the States. What they did sell was cigarettes, and since I was unsure of the next opportunity to visit Mompeo, I bought twelve packs.

The night was brisk; the air in the mountains becomes cold once the sun leaves the sky and the moon makes its appearance. Rebe, Katae, and I ventured to a small village to the north called Salisano. The annual jazz festival was taking place. A city on a hill built with stone and mortar a thousand years old, it was a stunning visual upon entering Salisano—the visible history pounded into the cobblestone, worn flat and smooth from generations of repeated use. The stones were uneven from wear and uniquely bowed from the repeated pressure. An astounding place, and as if this beautiful construction was just as common as a manufactured home in a trailer park, the inhabitants seemingly had no idea of it. Salisano was untouched by the mundanities of modernity and sat still for the living, outlasting another generation, and standing strong from the first day it was crafted. Nothing will ever knock over Salisano; it will be there long past my time on earth.

Electricity was probably a recent addition to Salisano, and while necessary, I yearned to see it in the light of a torch. The place where one would perch such a light was still on the side of a stone wall, fixture fitted, and appeared to be in working condition. The streets were winding and tight, so tight that no vehicle could fit through them. Vespa Mopeds were driven through them, carrying natives to their domains, and parked quaintly at the doorstep. One could easily become lost if not accounted for, as did I, stumbling drunk, taking in the music, and feeling as if, only for a moment, I fully appreciated it for what it was. It was as if I, too, lived in Salisano, waking every day, traveling to the bread maker, gardener, and butcher with a map seated inside my head, no need for traffic lights or local police, no desire for phones, as one could simply shout across the way and be heard throughout her high walls. Old men would pass; some seemed older than Salisano itself yet appeared stronger than most men. I fell in love with Salisano, and I still carry that love with me today. I will go back there one day, but that is for another time.

Katae said goodnight and went inside her house. Rebe and I began to move up toward our quarters, but she stopped. We were facing the vast expanse that we woke to every single day, but this time, light was only provided by the stars. We stared out into the abyss. She grabbed my hand and moved my arm over her shoulders. She was a foreign object so pleasantly placed underneath my Alkaline Trio sweatshirt.

During daylight hours, one could see wildlife working in conjunction with the valley—large hornets, the size of a BIC lighter, terrorizing the locals, establishing nests in olive trees, requiring fire for eradication, wild boars or jailbroken pigs lining the rim of the forest, preying on whatever source of food they could bring down, and the cherry tree I fell from on that warm June day. I almost broke my back for those cherries; they were traded for good conversation with a farmer down the way.

Without saying a single word, she stood there, breathing, looking out over the country, mesmerized, visually gorging on what was in front of her. I attempted to speak, and she shushed me. "Just look," she said. So, I did.

The valley was alive even at night, even in the thick darkness teeming with the life that would come from undercover at the sun's first break, almost lying-in wake, waiting for the light. I heard what the people of Fara Sabina heard one thousand years ago—a complete and utter cacophony of insects, the wind, and rocks under our feet, shifting slowly as we stood. Soothing is the sound of each natural noise when pieced together in mosaic. Fireflies flash brightly, attracting mates, and while they are ugly creatures up close, they are wonderous from far away.

Time moved slow in Fara Sabina—a pace I could get used to. In fact, time seemed to take on a new identity in the entire area encompassing Fara Sabina. The people seem to live forever, and I sincerely hope they do.

THE LAND

The Land is perfect. The imperfections are visible; one can hardly escape them. Rats travel together from dumpster to dumpster in refuse-littered alleyways. The homeless population thrives; the mentally ill run the streets at night. One would be given examples from time to time of why late-night train rides are to be avoided. I cared little for these precautions as I traversed neighborhoods in search of punk rock shows and the dirtiest 4:00 a.m. bar I could find. I moved in early August and faced a long winter. I appreciated the biting sting of her cold season; in fact, I quite enjoyed them. The grit of the South Loop shined when coated in ice, and the people seemed accustomed to short days, long nights, and single-digit temperatures. I lived in a dorm my first year at Roosevelt University. I had my own "apartment," cut off from others by virtue of a large steel door, but shared a bathroom with two other men about my age. This is where I met Stan, an ambitious young man from Cincinnati—"The Nasty Natti," as he would affectionately call it. Outside of our living quarters, I doubt we would have been friends, but I am quite grateful for the friendship we shared. We were both crude and vile in humor, sharing in the acrimonious critique of our peers.

Roosevelt was a higher learning institution built on the concept of social justice. I left there thinking I knew everything. I did not know how to run a business, but I felt I knew how to run a country. I was so sure I possessed all the knowledge I would ever need, and it was no thanks to my professors. I thought I was finished, but I was only just beginning.

Today, the only thing I know is that I know so little. Of what I am confident: music is magic, there is no greater touch than that of a woman, and there is pure innocence in children. I have a demon in my bones and an angel in my bloodstream. They wage war daily. My heart burns like a scorched-earth battlefield. I have the propensity for wickedness and the inclination for fondness. I am both the hero and the villain, the protagonist and the antagonist. I can choose to build a home or choose to burn it down.

Enduring the political fights that sour relationships or outright poison them, I have lost friends over opinions, winning battles and losing them. What is most regrettable is the love lost, the battles needlessly fledged as if to satisfy something, something not yet realized.

I used to hate men without ever meeting them. I despised those who dared to disagree, and, oh my, there were many. Wishing demise, giving no mercy, and granting no quarter. I have more in common with a man than I do with an idea, and while I used to die on many hills, I wish to share with the former, for we have much more to gain.

I want to learn, I want to feel, and I long to love in the process, for I am man living with both angels and demons.

It was safe to say that Stan and I had trouble finding others to comingle with and relate to. Luckily, we were of drinking age, so the city was entirely open to us. We ran around late at night, returning at all hours, stumbling in from the bar up the street, Exchequer. Many nights were spent there, buying overpriced beers and half-decent cheese fries. The whiskey was cheap, however, so I never complained. One Saturday, we smoked a full pack of cigarettes at the entrance and watched the Brown line pass overhead.

It was always so bitterly cold, as we were one block from Lake Michigan. I felt as though I was beginning to achieve whatever it was I set out to accomplish. I was hell-bent on living in the Land, escaping the small town where I was raised. What I loved most about the Land was the fact that lights were always on, no matter the hour. I could launch in four directions and find something to land on, something to do. Museums, parks, theaters, concerts, tours, conservatories, sporting events, and the Federal Reserve, for god's sake. Stan was instrumental in those days. He came from a good-sized city, hungry to experience, feel, and drink, just like me. Stan had lived in the Land for a year before we met. He taught me how to ride the trains and buses and how to navigate city streets. Lightly, we tussled through crowds, crossing bridges over the river. Stan and I were in search of good company.

I went to more concerts in those days than I ever have

and probably ever will. Live music was certainly the biggest motivator for moving to the Land, as several of my favorite bands lived there. I met members of bands that helped me through darker days, for which I am eternally grateful. I traveled many nights up north into Lakeview and Logan Square, or out west to West Town, Wicker Park, Roscoe, and Ukrainian Village. All had a distinct flavor, all coated in the grit that made me fall in love. I hear many cast aspersions on the Land, and they are all equally forgone, as you can tell me nothing of the Land I love. I was born there, not into life but into passion.

I saw the city as mine, I saw time as my own, and I would be unmoving in my desire to expand, to reach out further into my land and plant seeds wherever I wandered. Holding streets as landmarks and denoting them on my compass rose, the pavement was my playground, and the train was my jungle gym.

I love the train, a mixed bag of human souls entering and occupying any given car. Some headed places while others just rode to avoid the cold. All of us, at the same time, in the same place, if only for a moment. Once, a car on the Blue Line was infested with bedbugs and had to be bleached. Authorities at the CTA found it prudent to do this while the car was still underground, leaving the platform to reek of chemicals. These disruptions made the train more eventful to ride and gave it a sense of life as if the trains take the tracks of their own volition and are subject to the perils of life as are the riders. However, it still stands that whoever decided to put cloth seats on the Blue Line should be dragged down State Street for all to see.

One weekend in early April, Claire was in the Land for job

training, and we met at a bar downtown. We caught up on the usual particulars, and as the night went on, we became drunker and drunker. We hadn't seen each other since we kissed in my empty apartment before I departed for Italy. I spun her all the stories I had, sparing no detail, and I was grateful we had crossed paths again. I hadn't seen Claire in at least two years, and all at once, it was like we never parted, almost as if we were waiting for some fateful day in the future to rekindle whatever it was we had. I kissed her passionately, tasting of cigarettes and booze, and while she returned passion, we both knew we would soon be apart again, making it even more memorable. There are moments and memories that I cherish even though the ending is disappointing. Life is not a movie, and I hope it never becomes one. The cliché is true, as much as I may hate it.

The dorm, smack-dab on Wabash, was a self-imposed sentence that lasted nine months. Upon release, I had to find my own place to live. I landed on an apartment in Lakeview, off Clark, on Surf Street. I was close to the lake and near multiple train lines. A studio, quite small, it suited me nicely. I met a forty-five-year-old man, an Uber driver named Luis. He was a proud Puerto Rican, so proud, in fact, that he had at least three tattoos of the flag or some other insignia denoting his heritage. I found all Puerto Ricans in the Land to be quite proud of their home country, even those who were born in the United States. I felt at home in this air. I have always been proud of my Italian heritage, even if I'm only a half-blood. Luis was strong and had a bit of a past. He grew up in the Logan Square neighborhood before a new crowd moved in and filled it with overpriced tacos and irony for irony's sake. Luis would tell me of the gangs that used to run the streets, what blocks were controlled by whom, and where not to find yourself past sundown. He taught me the hand signs to flash if I ever encountered a certain type of person and the correct way to hang my fingers out of my pants pockets. I thought all these lessons superfluous, as times had changed, at least along the boulevard. The more I hung around with Luis, the more his roots showed. He had a story for every block, a memory for every corner, and he knew the best jibarito spot in the entire Land. Luis drove a Dodge Grand Caravan. He saw the van as an ideal vehicle, considering his job as a driver. He could fit up to eight, and this was helpful on nights in River North or with a group of partygoers anywhere in the Land. Luis loved to drive; he was authentic and would talk your ear off if you let him. Luis lived on Logan Boulevard, a block from the Eagle, amidst the million-dollar brownstones that used to sell for hundreds, and while those days were long gone, the history was apparent. The streets had a sense of something past and present.

Luis loved to smoke pot; he called it *mota*. We used to buy five-dollar bags of weed, drive around the Land, and smoke from a bat or a one-hitter. He had a whole system of implementation. A zipper pouch probably designed for headphones was his receptacle, perfectly sized to house the bat, a bag, and a lighter. If Luis saw one of the more attractive residents crossing the street, he would roll down his window and catcall them relentlessly. Luis was himself, often to a fault. Riding shotgun in that Dodge, I used to wonder what they thought of us. Quite the mismatch in terms of backstory and where we came from, but to us, it ceased to matter. We enjoyed one another's company, sharing many belly laughs, the type where I would struggle to breathe, eyes watering from laughter.

Luis had children, but he was only involved in the periphery of their lives. He was proud of them and wanted to make them proud. I think he did. His brother was high up in the Gangster Disciples, and he was eventually killed for it. After his brother's death, Luis found himself knee-deep in gang life. He did a couple of years for this or that charge and was strapped with a felony at a young age. This made job prospects difficult after he left gang life behind. He eventually started doing contractor work, fixing this or that; a bona fide handyman, he could fix nearly anything. We would sometimes visit his brother's grave or stumble upon the spot where he was murdered in the street. Luis didn't want that life, and I didn't want it for him, either. He was worth more than that.

People are worth too much to face death like a dog. Life is often more unforgiving than understanding, and once it is taken, there is no going back.

The environmental diversity left me to concentrate primarily on the Northside. I worked in a handful of restaurants, continuing my usual behavior in one form or another and acting in ways quite fitting for a creature of the night. I could be high and drunk and still perform the duties quite effectively. Restaurant work attracts low-quality people as well as high-quality people, but the latter is more unseen. Something about muscle memory and low ambition, reliance on the goodwill of patrons, and the obscurity in group responsibility. Counter service was ideal, as I even lacked the ambition to become a waiter in one of those fancy, expensive establishments.

I often wonder what the drummer thinks of me. We worked at a taco restaurant together, and although we seldom agreed on much politically, I liked to be around him. He was fresh, fun, and full of life. He was native and had an honest respect for Mother Nature, as did his forefathers, and it was no cheapened version. He was over six feet tall, with long hair that he often wore in braids. He was quite the budding fashion model, his face and physique covering the side of Nordstrom's downtown. He invested in his band, saving any money he could for touring. He loved reggae and Mexican music, to which he would sing along and howl when permitted. Rarely wearing a frown, he was as easygoing as they come and was measuredly kind toward others. Fashionable and expressive, I've incorporated much of his style into my own, especially ankle-length pants. He was racially ambiguous, but when he told you of his heritage, it seemed to make sense. We would often joke about his natural lack of facial hair, but I think he looked better without it. He traveled by bike even in the winter months, seemingly impervious to frigid, below-zero temperatures and the stinging of wind. He was the drummer in a band whose music I found enjoyable, regardless of his role in it.

I was a mess—wardrobe disheveled, requiring three hand-rolled cigarettes every hour. I would usually take three 20 mg Adderall XR capsules. Half the capsule was clear, and I liked to notice the little pearls dancing on the inside. We opened the restaurant together that winter and, side by side, appeared an odd couple. Preparing margaritas and parsing out salsa for the day, we shared many conversations, and while some were *deeper* than others, I enjoyed them all the same. He had a sense of calm about him, as if he was comfortable in his own skin and attempted to lend that feeling to others.

The Land holds many virtues and reasons to love, but there is also a lack of it, loss, and little remorse for the living. On one end, there is opulence, safety, and bright lights, while on the other, there are broken windows and crying mothers.

THE WATER'S EDGE

The night began with my usual trepidation toward social settings and riding the train as far north as I could imagine. Stan had just signed a lease on a new apartment, so, with reluctance and out of sheer boredom, I agreed to make the trek. I only went because Stan was my first friend in The Land. The apartment was nothing special.

Edgewater was completely foreign to me. I had only known it to exist because it was one of the stops on the Red Line, a route I studied like a textbook—simple to understand but nearly impossible to comprehend. I was ignorant of the vast expanses of a city that seemed to just bleed into more and more territory. Neighborhoods stretching blocks, spilling over into the next. I'm told they are clear-cut, with defined borders according to cross streets and multi-cornered intersections, but I failed to see the pattern. Trains barreling down hundred-year-old tracks, successfully moving people from one end of the city to the other. One can reasonably count on the trains to arrive on time and serve a purpose beyond transportation.

On a Friday in June, my second year in the Land, my dad informed me of my half-brother. Strange, this feeling—I was an only child growing up and still feel as though I am, but, in an instant, that fact changed. Nothing other than acknowledgment existed, as much remained the same. I seldom think of him; our eyes have never met, but I assume we share a likeness, as we are both our father's son—strong genetics, those Italians. My brother is a father, making me an uncle, adding another layer to this peculiar onion. We spoke once over the telephone and made plans to meet, nothing concrete, as he lives somewhere in San Francisco, but hearing his voice somehow connected me to the world. I was no longer space dust floating in the abyss. I had a connection, however small, to someone.

When I moved to the Land, I used school as an excuse. I was accepted to Roosevelt University, and that became an alibi of sorts. I made the mistake of living in a dormitory, a tall, rectangle-shaped building situated south on the twenty-second floor in the South Loop "neighborhood." After my first year, I exited the confines of dorm life, and the city presented itself in full exposure, appearing more open than ever. I walked blindly through experiences but felt comfortable enough in the dark. Much like my time spent in Italy, I imagined that I would be pushed into a current, confident not to let my head underwater.

Back at Edgewater, the night was perfect, one of those nights inmates clamor for. Short sleeves and short jeans were all I needed to brave a warm summer's night. It was mid-July, if memory serves, and the air smelled ordinary yet ripe with opportunity. Stan and I had an affinity for dive bars and the people they attracted. Cash only, screw-top bottles, cigarettes, and drunk conversations. We sat and ordered at the first quarter of the bar, dimly lit, music playing but not so loud, as you could still make out the spoken word. And then I saw her. Sitting alone, seemingly determined to partake in activities that Stan and I had set out for as well. I had taken no notice of her at first, as she was just another person in this enormous city whose story I would never know.

The light coming in over the water's edge was blinding. One must block a portion to see the subject clearly. She was a comet crashing through, a most delighted interruption. A shot and a beer sat in front of her, a half-full pack of American Spirit tobacco, and a single hand-rolled cigarette. While my initial impression would turn out to be partially incorrect, I doubt anyone could live up to the way she appeared to me in that moment.

Discovering love seems to be an instant, a flash, bulbs burst, an image captured forever. A single-minded drive to share a moment. My goal became to talk to her. Stan pumped fleeting courage into my spine, and I kept an eye on her. I waited like an alligator in the brush, on the edge of the water, lying completely still, aware that if she perceived any movement, it would be taken as a threat, and while she certainly may evade me, I had a smile to surprise her with. She began to move, taking a step toward the patio.

This was my moment to act. Other predators inhabit the environment, and they, too, stalk their prey. I drank my beer and positioned a pre-rolled cigarette, ready to light, attempting to appear natural, as if we serendipitously decided to step out at the same time. I stepped outside, and it was like stepping off a cliff. I imagine my face went white because my brain, right then, was completely empty. I struggled to offer a greeting; instead, I just stared, forcing her to acknowledge my presence and attempt to engage with the strange man in front of her.

She asked, "You need a light?"

I responded with words that, looking back, were purely instinctual, as there was no way I spoke on my own volition. She offered me a seat at the bench where she was sitting, which I accepted eagerly.

"I love the first drag, the crackling of paper, the flame engulfing the tobacco," she said, standing up.

"So, where are you from?"

"I'm from New Jersey," she said.

"Sure, sure, but where are you really from?"

"Oh, you can tell. Most people can't," she said, smiling sheepishly.

"You have a slight accent but not an obvious one, difficult to place, really. I find you to be quite special; you have a certain air about you," I said, shoving my entire foot in my mouth.

"Thank you. No one has ever said that about me."

"So, where are you from?" I asked.

I feared I was letting on too much, as I was suddenly aware of how comfortable she made me. It was almost as if I'd known her for years. She had something about her that, I think, is visible for all to see but may just live in my perception. Either way, I could not deny the fact of it, a fact so glaring that to ignore it would be an outright lie. I was enamored and willingly drew myself in.

"I can assure you, I'm nothing special," she said, laughing with a slight smile of self-deprecation.

"Maybe so. I'll be the judge of that," I added slyly.

We talked, smoked, and drank beers, and if he didn't come outside, I think I would have completely forgotten about my company, Stan.

"Hey, Jack, aren't you going to introduce me to your friend?"

"Yes, of course. This is uh . . . Alina," I stuttered over her name, my brain misfiring, encountering her as the first of its kind.

"Nice to meet you," said Stan, holding his hand out to shake.

"Likewise. So, you two are friends? Do you live together?"

"No, we used to. We met at school and lived in the same dorm. Stan here just moved into a new place around the corner."

I believe Stan could sense our desire to sit alone, as he bothered me for a smoke, which I provided, moving him along.

We met a cast of characters that night, some of whom went as far as to say that they were psychic and knew her and I were suddenly creating something. Strange how the psychic was correct, even in a drunken stupor. I remember hoping they were right because it was that moment that I knew she was made for me. It was in the way she spoke, in her construction and physique—she imparted something in me that evening. The person sitting in front of me was not *just* a person—I refused to believe she was ordinary. I thought that the world had yet to witness her. I had never felt such an overwhelming wave of emotion before, whether it be love or hate, fear or pleasure, sadness or jubilation. It was as if I came alive by it, as I was already born, but it wasn't until that night at the Double Bubble that I truly felt *alive*. Something inside me turned over like an engine.

I needed a piss, and when I returned, I noticed her Irish

exit. I immediately felt the urge to leave. I had only stayed past one drink because of the seismic shift that had taken place on the back patio. She was the sun crashing into my solar system, repositioning every planetary body that once made up my alignment. She was at the center; I was simply in orbit.

I left Double Bubble, walked to the train, bringing along a half-full beer I smuggled out as a parting gift. I was an actor in those old 1920s movies, dancing down the street in a top hat and cane.

I gave her my number the night we met, so if she was so inclined, she would know where to dial. The next night, it happened. I was immeasurably pleased when her New Jersey area code invaded my phone in the early evening. We settled on meeting at a bar on Irving Park near my tattoo artist's shop. I knew the area well, so I served as her guide. She was a bit late, and as I would later learn, she was just never ready on time, entirely something I could overlook, as I was burning to see her. We shot Jim Beam and drank from long-neck bottles; she even rolled me a couple of her cigarettes. We roamed Ashland to the surrounding bars and had a couple hits and a couple misses. It wasn't until the end of the night that we found ourselves on yet another back patio, as if this was just any night we would spend together on any given Saturday in the Land. Once again, we spoke freely, no pretense or act, just the slow drop of a veil.

She started, "Do you ever feel stuck? A stuck like how there is no give in any direction. Imagine you're caught in a web, and the more you move, the more you're trapped."

"Do you feel stuck?" I asked.

"Sometimes. I like my job, but I want a new one. I like New Jersey, but I want to move. These constant contradictions that just seem to live inside my mind—I don't know, it's just a lot sometimes."

At this point in the night, we were both inebriated but still in control of our faculties, quite enjoying the company. Ten Cat announced last call, and if measured in minutes, the night passed quickly. We left the bar and sat at a concaved entrance to a neighboring apartment building. We fumbled along, and our lips met. The flowers bloomed at once in midsummer, the trees grew an inch taller and extended further, reaching toward the sky, and the moon shone brighter. In an instant, the chaos ceased to exist. The rotten stench of the Land and grime-coated streets were suddenly a world away. After several minutes of contact, her Uber arrived to take her further north to her aunt's apartment. It was nearly 3:00 a.m., so the Brown Line had shut down for the night, or the next train was over thirty minutes away, both of which were possible. Ordering an Uber to take me several blocks south to my apartment, I would crash into bed with little regard for anything except that evening playing inside my head.

She was in the Land visiting her aunt on her annual summer trip. She had one week left of her two-week excursion. We spent the whole week together, lying naked in the dark, talking, and learning about each other. All the things we held back would eventually come out, but the information volunteered created a mutual vulnerability. I found that my love for her was building, word by word and touch by touch. To feel it grow was like witnessing a miracle.

The moonlight crept into my studio apartment, illuminating the lines that cut her out against the backdrop of light. We were completely exposed and immensely comfortable. I wanted to see her faults and imperfections, but I struggled to find them amidst the angelic nature of her body. She did and does contain many flaws, but in that week, she appeared perfect to me. She spoke of them. I didn't need the truth, but I didn't want a lie. This human in front of me was seemingly perfect but volunteered to share her flaws; she offered them as an attempt to discount from her image. It was almost as if she knew how I saw her; she was trying to paint the picture that would make me weary, but I was far from dissuaded. The promotion of her faults brought her down to size, and her voluntary exposure showed how much she cared about thoughtful articulation and accurate communication. She was subject to the hardship and wounds one acquires simply by living life, and knowing this afforded us a certain sense of commonality.

We were loving in limited time. The impending day of her departure served as the ceiling or the demarcation of our finite time together. When Alina and I had unlimited time, we squandered it, becoming souls I hardly recognized.

She established a belief in me that, even when dragged through mud, beauty is inherent and unbothered by circumstance. Although the subject may be blind to it, the illustrations are at the forefront and cannot help but take center stage. In other words, those few who are objectively beautiful, even when unaware, exist in standard deviations away from the mean. She will never shed her beauty or outfit it. One does not know it but is rather a witness to it. No man can control or harness it, and it is exactly the temptation toward it that drives man. Men yearn for it and can truly never attain it; the fact that it exists in so few forces man to pursue it. The simple scarcity that makes her special is a gift from something beyond the natural world, and while I'm no mystic, she became my muse. She was as special as the sun setting in the west, bursting with color, fuchsia and purple, shades of blue, and burning orange, one hue mixing and dyeing with the next, the sun shining through wavelengths and entering the eye just before the earth crosses into shade. Rather than the sun vacating our plot, she was there in the dark, the whites of her eyes becoming a source of both light and warmth.

I worked a terrible job in those days, waking up at 4:30 a.m. to take a train to Gold Coast. I wanted her to stay there and be in my home when I returned. She did, and we would laugh about how, if she wanted, she could have fleeced my entire apartment. I wasn't worried; I hardly had a thing. On her last night in the Land, I could tell she didn't want to go. I didn't want her to go either because I knew that as quickly as she came into my life, she would be out of it. The day of her departure, she gathered her things from her aunt's and came over before her flight. She seemed unfazed by the implications of heading back to New Jersey. She said she would call me if she got bored, and I perceived it as a polite way of saying, "This is it, kid." She walked out of the threshold to my matchbox apartment and into the hallway. I remember thinking that I should chase after her to tell her how I felt, how I never wanted to be apart from her again. This was not an action I chose, so I began to think of how sad the prospect made me.

My phone rang one time that night, and it was her. We talked for hours. It was the beginning of a long and perilous pursuit of creating something out of only a voice. This didn't stop her, though, and it surely didn't stop me. That day when she left, she called me to continue our time together as if she never left. It's almost like her life in New Jersey was held on standby, and in the Land, she lived completely. We lived together, even though we were one thousand miles apart. We talked for hours on the phone about the weather or her childhood in Russia and Syria. We played stupid word games over FaceTime. We would share answers to profound questions about life or the future. I felt entirely empty when we were apart. I slipped hard in those days. I found myself unable to function, and my time was spent on wild assumptions about who she was spending her time with. The idea that someone else had her broke me, and the thought of another man viewing her in the half-light cut me at the knees. I was desperate for any inkling of her activity and became paranoid about how she chose to spend her time. The feeling was not basic jealousy but rather an hourglass slowly spilling sand. As each grain spilled, I risked her slipping away, spending her free time with others. I pictured the grains dramatically dropping, the risk increasing with each drop of grain. The feeling reflected my own perceived inadequacies. How could I demand that she love me when I had no love even for myself? How was I not entirely consumed by this winter? Maybe I was, but the very nature of being consumed leaves no mile marker, and up until then, it went unnoticed.

Long stretches of self-destruction were only interrupted when she would visit me, or I would visit her. After one month, I decided that it was time to see her. Several hours every day on the phone seemed like an appropriate enough reason to buy a plane ticket and surprise her. We would spend a weekend close to the city and do whatever we wanted. I liked visiting her because it meant being in her element, seeing the places where she grew up after coming to America at age eleven. She showed me her old apartment building in Midtown and shared stories of the outright debauchery she and her friends created. She talked about her old roommate who smoked cigarettes with the windows closed and some old mutt she cared for. She showed me her favorite bars, and we explored some she never patronized. We visited the Met, MoMA, and the Guggenheim. One night in Brooklyn, we fucked in the bathroom of a pool hall. She loved fucking in public. Call it a kink, or maybe she wanted to spice up her climax.

We would stay somewhere different each time I visited. Once in Brooklyn and twice in Jersey City. We braved the cold winter together and shared warmth indoors until, inevitably, I would depart from her or she from me. She would occupy my mind until the next occasion when I could see her. She visited the Land often as well and even overstayed a work trip once, from which she was subsequently fired. We were inseparable on those occasions, and if only for a moment, I thought I had a taste of what life with her could be like.

"I'm not sure if I'm one of those people who can stay married forever. I imagine that I'll be a divorcée one day. Whoever he is, I'm sure we would have a good relationship, but I lose feelings fast, and things turn platonic. We would be linked, as I also imagine we would share children."

"How can you know that?" I asked.

"I'm not sure. Call it intuition or just pessimism concerning the future," she replied.

Standing naked in the bathtub, sharing a cigarette, I

attempted to dig deeper.

"Well," I said, "what if you meet somebody and everything works out? Like, what if you never split up?"

"You don't actually believe it works like that, right?"

"Maybe, maybe not. I guess I'm not really sure."

She began, "Think about your parents. Did you think they would ever end their marriage? I mean, sometimes, things that seem so secure are the first things to go when the water moves. We're all just floating in water."

"Sure, but nothing is preordained. Can't you just wait to see what happens before taking such a strong position?" I countered.

What she said next really threw me, as I had yet to understand her fully and quite possibly never did.

"I'll be dead by twenty-eight. I saw a fortune teller once, and she told me I'd be dead by the time I turned twenty-eight."

That was the thing about her—she was so sure of some things yet so sheepish in others. She was ripe for contradiction but not the kind that questions character.

It was 3:00 a.m., and snow flurries began to fall. There was no screen on the window we smoked from; my hand nearly froze from hanging over the ledge. I wrapped my free hand around her navel and brought my body closer to her backside. I was a whole head taller than her. I could comfortably rest my chin on the top of her head, as we seemingly fit perfectly together. The comforter draped over my shoulders fell all around her, offering protection from the wind. We stared out over the back-alley behind my building, a view which I saw daily, but with her there, it somehow appeared different, almost new. She turned, faced me, and dug herself into my chest. I threw our half-smoked cigarette out of the window, and we fucked in the bathtub by the light of the streetlamp.

I had decided to move after my lease expired at the Surf Street apartment building—a beautiful old building that, while showing age, had an air of sophistication. The marble floors met my stuttered steps leading to the main staircase, where I took many tumbles. Frequent encounters with neighbors and the foyer chandelier virtually demanded I become more accustomed to the alleyway entrance. Those stairs were tighter and resembled more of a spiraling staircase, an entrance less fitted for a stumbling drunk.

I once forced a bed frame down that staircase, inebriated and near blackout. I busted and broke the pieces meant to connect the side frames, making them trusted and sturdy, forcing the structure to collapse with ease under my will. The staircase, however, posed a greater difficulty. The pieces were awkward, and I couldn't see straight. I remember propping myself up on the handrail to acquire leverage while my lower half forced downward, pushing and sweating, as I had been a stranger to physical exertion beyond trips to the liquor store. The time and place were unfitted to my desire, but I pushed it, moving it inch by inch, scratching and damaging the walls, moving further down out of sheer will and a disregard for the conditions. I never considered working with the pieces of the frame, only against them, until one of us was too overworked. I eventually conquered my opponent; I left it there beside the dumpster without care or attention to the obstacle it posed for passersby, pieces strewn about, blocking the walkway. I gingerly hopped back up the two flights, out of breath and drunk, purposefully unaware that I now had only a single mattress on a painfully single floor.

My feet felt like cemented blocks in those days. Moving not to advance or progress but only to see tomorrow. No direction and little ambition made for self-destructive ends. The means were inexpensive and centrally located. I would traverse those stairs only to revisit them minutes later and not again embark until the well ran dry. I often wondered if my unlucky neighbors could detect the smell of burnt tobacco, but maybe the window in my shower prevented detection.

I wrecked that apartment one night. I toppled my bookcase, damaging several bindings of which I still own. I smashed whatever was closest to me, and given the square footage of the apartment, most things were within arm's reach. I skipped my classes at Roosevelt the next day and attempted to rebuild after leveling the apartment.

I carried on through the days with a spotty attendance record, pursuing a degree I long gave up on. I spent most days alone save the extended weekends in New Jersey with Alina. When we were apart, I ceased to live. This is a state that, for man, is impossible to sustain, and the winter after we met chilled me to the bone. Loneliness consumed me. I turned to alcohol to try and soak up the pain from her lack of presence and my own inability to multitask. Was I so unaware that I could have both? Could I miss her greatly and still function as myself? Those feelings I projected onto her came from my shortcomings and inability to be independent once her stimulus was introduced. My spiraling wasn't enough to deter her from me. She announced she was moving to the Land in early April, claiming it was for a change of scenery, but I think we both knew it was so we could be together, or at least I did.

I was sitting on a train, heading to work at a job I hated more than the last, but it paid better, so I stuck with it. It was my birthday, and up until 4:00 p.m., I had not heard from her, which was out of the ordinary.

She planned to move two weeks later. I then found myself scrambling to prop up my lifeless apartment enough to pass as a potential home for her. I was walking on air for those two weeks. The very idea of her present, at nearly all times, was enough to move my body. I shook the rust off, as I was none the worse for wear. Each day was like a slow countdown. If it was a Tuesday, I need only to make it to Wednesday, and then Thursday after that. She showed up with bags in hand and a suitcase dragged behind her. She could have stayed with her aunt, but she chose to stay with me in my shoebox of an apartment. Before she found a job, she was home every day when I came home, and I truly felt content. I truthfully felt that if she was with me, it was all I needed to deal with the particulars that bog down a person's life, all of which can be too heavy a burden to carry sometimes. With her, I felt invincible, like the world was ours; we would share it and feast on the bounties yet to be discovered. A night in or a night out had all the same benefits. She was here—I could reach out and touch her. I could say her name, and she would look at me with those big eyes and perfect lips, mouthing letters in the arrangement that formed my name. The sound entered my ears, and her voice bounced around inside my heart. She was real, she was mine, and I was hers.

My lease was up on June 1, and I had found a larger apartment in Avondale prior to her move. Much to my displeasure, this location created hurdles concerning work and play. Talking it over and taking into consideration that we adopted a puppy, we needed to move not only into a different apartment but an entirely different neighborhood. We decided on Bucktown. Rent was less expensive than the surrounding area, and the apartment was ideal. It was the location we needed and was conveniently across the street from an enormous graffiti piece on the side of a cabaret bar. It was here that our relationship took a turn for the worse, and we fell ungraciously between friendship and hatred. The love we once shared turned into a shell of what it used to be. The flowers that once bloomed now lay dead, rotten, bending at their base, roots screaming to be assured. The trees that shot toward the sky were flattened by the force of cascading contempt. The environment once hospitable to us was now a barren wasteland with not even a mirage to quiet the death knell.

WESTERN AND MCLEAN

She sits atop a stoop with four descending stairs
built for a home that does not belong to her; quite possibly, this
is her sanctuary, her patch of reprieve from the unforgiving
pavement. One could hardly say she lives in the neighborhood;
one, however, could say she is alive. She wears a dusty, sweat-
stained cap, concealing strands of matted hair and a scalp
ridden with lice. Shoulders bare, she wears a spaghetti-strap
shirt held on by a single spaghetti. Under her shirt are two
large, rotund breasts, unsupported, revealing themselves
with any sudden movement. The force of gravity is unkind to
those who have nothing to catch them. A winter jacket tied
in a tangled knot is draped around her waist. This worn-out
garment and the contents of its pockets make up most of her
fleeting possessions; retention is impossible when one cannot
maintain their mind. A single black trash bag, appearing to be
industry-grade, serves as pants, with two holes in the bottom

cut wide enough to shove her portly legs. What was left of her fingerless gloves covered her unkempt palms. Her dry, cracked digits extended through the gloves, revealing black and green inch-long nails. She eats from a Styrofoam takeout tray, her fingers serving as her utensils. Her shoes are worn beyond repair. The tongues flayed out, no laces to keep them together, they are a size too small.

I love her.

Not the sort of love man has for another who excites passions or exemplifies values but for what we have in common. I have no idea how old she is. The caked-on grime appears to age her out of any reasonable estimation. She looks through me passing by on my way to the liquor store for the second time before sunset. She smiles, her bottom eyelid curves upward toward the top, and her pupils remain uncovered, as large as nickels, glossed over, looking but unseeing. I had been up since the sun rose and failed to say goodnight to the sky's last moon. I am a mess. I can't walk straight. I wear sunglasses to conceal my bloodshot eyes. The liquor store attendants know me by name and my dog as well. I cross Milwaukee and Western to Bucktown Liquors with the train rushing overhead. I have the same order every day.

"A pint of Jim Beam."

Or maybe a fifth, if the night required it. I pass her on my way back home, again across Milwaukee and up Western, until I reach McLean. She is always there, and I am too. She seems ever so content in her squalor, in her abject filth, lacking any care for the rat's nest she calls a body, for we both care little of our respective selves. What separates us is money, occupation, housing, matters of luck, mental health, a base of support, and preferred genetics. Dumb fucking luck that a small-town kid, who by all measures should have his shit together, is not in the same crashing current that she finds herself thrashing in. You see, I have laces in my shoes.

I pass her often, always offering a smile or a half-assed attempt at cordiality. On some days, she seems more present than others, and even though I try, I feel no better than those who look away when confronted with her presence. Many see her and offer no helping hand, not even a look of remorse or sorrow for her position. Indifference is commonplace in a metropolitan city as large as the one we share. Trim options when a person unfit for this world is thrusted into the reality of circling the drain. Should I offer my shirt? I have many and some I rarely use, clothing I wouldn't notice once gone or misplaced. Should I offer a few dollars for a warm meal, presumably the product of a fast-food grease trap? What good would that do? How much sustenance can be derived from a single meal? I cannot bring this woman home, as I am unwilling, and the coldness of Alina would indeed be extended in the invitation. She requires love, which I am in no position to give, as I am fresh out even for myself.

As many others do, I find it advantageous to pass with discontent and harbor a pinch of bitterness, pretending she doesn't exist, adding to the refuse that plagues the streets outside of manicured lawns and six-foot iron gates. So ironic that beauty exists in such a soiled soul. One must wash her multiple times to find it, but I know it is there. She lives; therefore, she is worthy of redemption, but the burden that entails retrieval is more cumbersome than the redemption I seek. I find it easier, not by choice but by the lack of will, to let another one go by the way of physical rot. There is great difficulty in mustering courage; ignoring one's conscience is more pleasing in the short run.

One year later, I imagine she occupies the same space, as the alternative is much to bear and seemingly all too common. What is most tragic is that there is but one conclusion, enveloped in addiction and mental illness. There are seldom those who receive the help they need. Truthfully, death is the preferable outcome, as the life she leads is not sought even by those who live it. I suppose life and death are relative, but the fact remains that life ought to be lived. The desire to change or to improve one's position must come from within them. No amount of effort can change a man who is unwilling to change himself. No amount of money or goodwill can cure a disease brought on by the self, a mind gripped in addiction. Man is not suited to rely on himself solely, however, and is quite ill-equipped to seek and ask for the help he needs. After all, there is comfort in a slow death, for there exists a sliver of freedom in indulgence.

Still, like the walls of my life during that time, they close in fast, and before long, the suffocation becomes adaptable, and life finds a way. It's quite simple, really. Carry on or die. But how one carries on is not so simple; life continues, or it does not, and in moments such as these, for this degraded woman carries on, carries on, on Western and McLean.

GOING BACK AND COMING BACK

I went back to southeastern Washington after conflicts in the Land became too much to bear. Alina was out of control with anger, and I was spiraling out from incessant drug use. I left the Land knowing I would return to her, but it was clear, we needed a break. We both drank Jim Beam until we could no longer stand, and after we sat, the fighting ensued. I felt as though everything was entirely fucked, so I went home for six weeks. Looking back now, I have no idea what I was thinking. The coke and booze were killing me, and we were doing a stand-up job of killing ourselves. There was no amount of time that could remedy our ills.

My good friend Vincent, in southeastern Washington, lost his girlfriend to a fentanyl overdose a week prior to my return. She was a close friend, and it pains me to speak in the past tense. The world was less bright, the sun noticeably dim as I sat at the Western Blue Line Station reading the text message announcing her death. Vincent did everything a person can do. He shook a drug habit, but he couldn't do it for her. He used to tell me she was the sunshine type. She was a sparkle in his eye before and after the drugs. I have known Vincent since we were fifteen, and before her, I had never seen him light up like a flame you see in oil fields, always burning and always fed. She did something to him, the something that happens to a man in love. He burned and had a constant source of fuel. She was his energy, and he matched it with intense veracity. I arrived the day before her funeral and attended out of both respect and earnest disbelief. Unfortunately, grief can cause the strongest of minds to bend and break, and those left in the wake of her untimely death placed their anguish at Vincent's feet. An ugly thing to do, if one is to imagine the passing of a loved one, there can be nothing gained by holding the innocent accountable. They'll offer their earnest apologies later in life, but that does no good for him now. I wish my hugs and company were enough for him; I like to think her ghost accompanies him, as I know she would have promised it. They shared a love that was above explanation. She loved him with all her heart, and he loved her forever. Drugs take hold of people, and the blues grabbed them. The thing most upsetting is to know that while her death devasted the lives of those around her, it was exactly those who felt responsible. Her loved ones pushed him out and created more heartbreak than was necessary, an excess well of pain and suffering fed by those most affected. The passing of a loved one forces those closest to question what they could have done. "If only I would have called her more or stepped in."

Hate is a mask worn only by grief. It is far easier to blame a scapegoat or personify the thing that killed her when the perished are to blame. Stints in rehab and the outpouring of support an addict may receive is miniscule if the drive to use is greater. She had all the love in the world; she was magnetized, pulling in those around her. Fentanyl is poison; I've felt it myself, and it should never be touched. I don't like drugs that could kill me in one shot; I prefer the slow decline, the gradual breakdown. Human beings are driven to find answers to the questions that plague them, when, often, there is no reason, nothing to blame except natures' indifference to life.

I returned to Washington in an attempt to clean up my mess of a mind. The first day went well, but I spent the rest of the time fucked up and facedown. About a day in, I was once again away from Alina, my mind reverting to the place it had been when we first met. I was living in the fear and paranoia about who she was seeing and the sex she was having. Whenever we were apart, she wanted an open relationship. I imagine this was to survey the landscape unencumbered by my prying eyes. We both fucked other people when we were apart, but it always made me feel sick. I hated fucking other people because it meant she was too, and the thought was disgusting. I found that I always felt bad about it. I was only fucking strangers so she wasn't the only one having a fuck. I lied when she asked about it. She seemed to get off on the thought of her boyfriend fucking someone else, and while many men might enjoy the notion, I despised it. She never lied, as she was honest to a fault. She cared little for the way her actions or words affected others. Maybe this helps clear a cloudy conscience and destroy pretenses, but either way, it is an enviable pathology. I think she enjoyed it and was quite proud of herself.

I am from a small town, mostly known for its wine

and wheat fields. Largely, the town is devoid of life. Senile geriatrics outnumber those under forty at least two to one, and the contrast is glaring. Retirement communities exist in high numbers and consume entire swathes of land, creating an ever-present feeling of certain and impending death. The town moves at a snail's pace and knows no life past sundown. There are a handful of bars, none worth mentioning, all equally generic and more akin to highway sports bars than they are to gathering places where one can meet others of a similar age. To be there, in that town, a young man or woman is suffocated and soul sucked. Art is completely absent, especially in places that claim to be creative. There are two hundred wineries, where tourists descend and leave little for the long term, rest stops on their journey to quench an insatiable thirst. This town is a waiting room. Meaningless conversations with unimpressive residents paint the streets gray and eat life alive. These residents imbibe the world through television screens or digital articles reciting the danger of larger cities. Residents here feel safe in their desperate attempts to control nature, nothing wagered, nothing lost, ignorant that to be alive is to be in danger. The residents here risk nothing, pursuing mediocrity. As good as dead, they stare blankly at an unchanging landscape, an entirely predictable existence made up of baby births and the changing of seasons.

Of the more excitable class, there exists a heavy presence. Of those injured by my words, I venture the proposition that you are not of whom I speak. There exists much life in those who choose to live it. I've seen wine cellars belonging to a couple full of life; they are welcoming and yearn for time well spent. To smile and to laugh is all one can ask. They yearn deeply.

Time spent in desired company is hardly regrettable, and often, all one needs is a night of wine and genuine smiles. I do not hate the people of my hometown; I just wish them more. I wish them the prestige of hardy character and the acknowledgment of sturdy spines.

I was back in the place I was born, miserable and blaming bad times on everything except myself. I felt I was overweight and wanted to lose my booze belly before going back to the Land. I would never give up booze, so I gave up carbs instead. I drank bourbon neat and required no chaser. One night, I had about seven or eight bourbons at The Orange and walked home when the night appeared over at 11:00 p.m. I stumbled on the block leading down dark streets, passing by weeds growing from concrete, my path lit by porch lights. I passed the park where I had sex once in the parking lot and ate mushrooms under the gazebo. I was a pioneer, lost and wandering. I walked on sidewalks made of grass and managed to fall once or twice. I ate the pavement, and my phone slipped from my shirt pocket. I got up and continued walking, and upon noticing the loss, I returned to the scene, vision doubled and shaky from dark water. I looked thoroughly but came up empty. I had a little over halfway to go, and I felt something break inside me. I needed my phone but not really. I had no one to call and expected no calls, but the void was present and screaming.

I decided to steal a car.

When I wake up after a night of heavy drinking, my mistakes rush in all at once. My face in a grimace and eyes slanted, I recall the actions I regret. Like being in a boxing match, I try to defend, but the memories, however blurred, always find my chin. On this night, I risked auto theft and a DUI charge. My line of thinking held that if I can make it to my house quickly, I can get to my car and then retrieve my phone, no harm, no foul.

I tried one car door, and it was open—convenient, quick, no alarms blaring, and not a soul in sight. I entered the vehicle, and the keys were seated nicely in the ignition, almost begging to be turned. I started the Mazda, and she roared like a lion. Drunk and near blackout, I drove as I always do, orderly and law-abiding. The trick to drunk driving is to know that you are drunk, and drive as you normally would. Follow the left line and be careful to stay inside it. Do not speed or take chances, as you will eventually pay. Remember to signal and keep eyes on the road even when doubled. Understand that to achieve objectives, one must be consistent, and there is little consistency found in a DUI. Pay attention to the lights and street signs, and most importantly, keep your eyes peeled for Jake.

After driving about five blocks, I parked the car a block from my house, left the keys where I found them, and carried on to the next part of the plan. I walked home, grabbed my keys, and was off. I drove back to the scene of the first crime and searched for my phone. I was too drunk to stand, so I gave up and returned home. I needed the bright summer sun to locate it. I returned in the morning and found it placed nicely in the grass, waiting to be plucked. No missed calls, no missed texts, I risked it all to retrieve it, and there was nothing to show for it other than the phone itself. Maybe I expected Alina to call, but why the hell would she do that?

I told my friends about my adventures, and they laughed wholeheartedly. I realized my proclivity to risk and the lack of control I have of myself sometimes. None of it mattered, as I was on my way back to the Land the next day. Coming back or going back or whatever the hell I did was a feeble attempt to change, a half-assed effort to restore what I thought I was losing.

I returned to the Land, and my energies were blazing. I was back. I was ready to pick up where I left off. My drug dealers hadn't forgotten about their number-one customer, and Pedro at the liquor store still knew my name.

Alina and I painted over the past and began again. A fresh coat in a different color, but the bottom layer just bled through. I had habits to kick, and she had anger to control. They were two problems stemming from the same issue, and both of us were equally obstinate. I had no desire to change, even though I said I did, and she never knew the full picture. From a lack of honesty, I filled the canvas with too much of not enough. What she needed of me, I was unwilling to give. I needed to consider both sides of our story and, instead of speech, focus on action. She wanted what most women want, a secure environment where we can grow from a company to a crowd and realize a sense of family. Those two things were precisely the types I was unable to give, as I was hanging on by a thread, and often, that thread would snap only to be hemmed and dangling again.

During this time, I was trying my hand at stand-up comedy and became obsessed with the art. Joey Diaz was playing the theater. It was late October. Alina had a friend, Jasmine, visiting from New York. She was staying at our apartment for a few days. Benny, Jasmine's lover, was in the Land, playing a show at Chop Shop, one of the many stops where the tour took him and his band. I left for the theater at about 6:00 p.m., my face full of coke. I rode the Blue Line east to Washington and walked the couple of blocks to State Street. There was light rain, headlights from passing vehicles reflected off the puddles, and I could feel the Land pulsating. I arrived at the theater, jumped in line, and smoked a cigarette. I had a few drinks at the bar and a couple bumps in the bathroom once the gates opened. After Joey said goodnight, I set out west for Chop Shop. Benny played bass and sounded good enough to afford the band a decent following. Benny and his band partied like I do; we got along swimmingly. An eclectic bunch, each with their own style and personality, together on stage, they were one.

I arrived and Alina greeted me with a face full of coke. She embraced me, kissing me all over, wearing that smile to make me melt. She was in her element when surrounded by loud music and packed venues. She was a creature of the night, and amidst the flashing light, she appeared flawless. We climbed the stairs to the green room, where I met them all at once. The names fleet quickly; they mean much less than faces. Presented with a mirror and a supple mound of coke, I found myself face deep in a pile of powder. I can work a room, and so can Alina. We enjoyed acting as if our relationship was perfect. We loved to present, lying in real time. We looked good together. She was obviously the star, but I like to think I complimented her nicely. After Chop Shop closed, we went to the band's tour bus and talked shit for twenty minutes. Benny and Jasmine sat affectionately on the bus, telling stories and holding court. They were a wild couple, temperamental but loving. Jasmine had trust issues due to the success of Benny's band, and I really can't blame her; musicians do have a certain reputation. Alina and I sat close on the couch opposite them, and for once, we were in tune. After a couple shots and a couple lines, we went across the street to Flatiron where Alina and I dominated in darts and had our asses handed to us in pool. We weren't done with the night, and Lito had just arrived, delivering another package for us. We passed the bag around, paid the tab, slammed the beers, and set out.

We all stumbled down lively blocks, leading to the steps of Danny's Dance Room. There is a large disco ball that hangs from the ceiling and never fails to mesmerize. Alina and I danced, or more accurately, I *tried* to dance. She moves with the music as she always does, her limbs lightweight, flowing like the subtle swing of a wind chime. She never misses a step, allowing the beat to guide her. The only time she ever gives herself over completely is on the dance floor. There is safety on the floor, and she dances with a confidence others wish they had. I paid cash and bought several rounds for her and our friends. The time was 3:00 a.m. or so when we exited Danny's. The air was brisk but not so much to cause a chill. It was fall in the Land, and the leaves were starting to change. In a few short weeks, the deciduous trees would break the stems extending from their branches and leave leaves collecting in the gutter. Benny and I walked our women to the apartment and sang along the way. We had similar music tastes and embarrassed ourselves while gallivanting down the street.

We all arrived, and the hostility immediately followed. Alina always found a way to fight, but in front of her friends, she remained pallid and unnerved. I felt closer to her than most nights, and suddenly, she dissolved in the smoke of her temper. I can't imagine I had my wits about me, and even if I did, I know I waffled, drunker than those around me. I cared more to entertain and failed to be a base for her. Our company left for their rental, none the wiser as she saved her disdain for later.

A month later, through a patch of bumps and bruises, we found ourselves in the frequent care of Alina's six-year-old cousin, Anya. Alina's aunt, Sonya, was a single mother, and other than lacking the presence of a man, one did not suspect she lacked anything other than time. Alina and I were there to pick up Anya from school, and I remember playing a game of tag, where I happily surrendered a win. I ran backward, backpedaling, watching her run as fast as she could. Her blond hair waving in the wind, her smile missing teeth yet so uncompromisingly pure, the three of us held hands and walked north toward the Red Line. A primal sort of mindset seeped in. I felt protective of her; any perceived threat venturing close enough would have their throat cut with the inside of my house keys.

The Lincoln Park Zoo had their Halloween theme up and running, a popular spot for adults and children alike. Alina, Sonya, Anya, and I met at the zoo one fall day to explore and partake in festivities. I gave Alina and her aunt some much-needed respite, as single motherhood is nothing to be taken lightly. Anya and I journeyed through the small corn maze. I lost her a few times. If it wasn't for her uncontrolled laughter at an unreasonable volume, I think I would have grown concerned. I chased her through the twisting and turning of cornstalk, winding and shuffling through other explorers feebly attempting to keep up with our pace. She was a wild animal laughing and tripping every ten feet. She seldom cried, but when she did, I would scoop her up into my arms and say, "I got you. I got you."

We exited the corn maze and found Alina and her aunt in what seemed like vigorous discussion. Apparently, the Russian language, an expressive tongue, sounds more aggressive than it is. I have no idea what the words mean, which forces me to pay greater attention to the speaker. The words move like a roller-coaster cart, drawn out and long. There is a fullness of sound, a steady progression toward the point that is both desired and impending. Anya ran up to her mother and exploded on her with a smile and hug, nearly knocking her off her chair. Alina shot a look at me and smiled so wide I thought it was going to jump on mine. For a moment, I felt that she loved me.

Most nights around the holiday season, Alina and I picked up Anya from school. Alina's aunt was working at the hospital and was still in possession of her keys, so before taking Anya home, we first needed to retrieve them. Alina took the elevator to her aunt's floor, and I waited with Anya in the lobby. Through Anya's eyes, the Christmas tree was enormous and perfectly set by a corner window, lit up brightly with lights and ornaments. She ran to it in a full sprint. I held her up so she could take a better look at the tallest and widest tree she'd ever seen. I set her down and turned around to find a woman in scrubs who was kind enough to take a picture.

"Would you like me to take a picture of you and your daughter?" she asked.

"She's not . . . sure, thank you," I said.

I hesitated in my reply because I had never been considered, or considered myself to be anything close to resembling a father, but in that moment, I was pleased by the mistake. Anya was a handful and gave many fits, but she was perfect. She was untouched by the world; the indifferent nature of humanity had yet to notice her, leaving her to be but a flower in bloom. Wearing only pajamas or an Elsa outfit, she was entirely unencumbered by the gaze of onlookers, so completely free to smile and laugh at anything amusing. Anya was not my own, but I would die for her if the conditions demanded. I would throw myself in front of the Red Line if it meant protecting her. The world is an unsafe place for even the strongest of men—it consists primarily of those uncompassionate and eager to break a heart. An inherent evil quite accompanies the uncontaminated, eventually spoiling us all. I began to take on the sense that, even in my own misgivings and inability to stand up straight, I could possibly absolve myself if it was for her. I had suddenly found a purpose, and however small of a role I played in her life, she will always have me for whatever she may need, even if she doesn't know it.

The nurse and I exchanged pleasantries as she handed my phone back. There is no way for her to know what she had done for me that night, and I hope to pay it forward one day. I still have that photo, and I look at it whenever I feel sad or lonely. I can transport myself back to that event if only for a moment. There's something so clean in the face of a child, something that the world and society will eventually distort and suck dry, but the picture I have of us captures the unalloyed smile, the face of one who has done no harm and, in fact, has done nothing but love. Sometimes, I felt that if Alina could see the way I cared for Anya, she might be tempted to succumb to children and matrimony. My proclivity for drugs and booze was surely a downside and probably a most glaring disqualifier. I thought that I would surely give that all up if it meant having a child with her. When we were all together, I felt close to being an actual man, a possible father figure for a girl who didn't have one. I am the great faker, and she was young enough to buy the bullshit. There was something in the way of being needed; this child would run to me if she got a knot in her dress or was too tired to walk farther. She would stare up at me with those innocent eyes, and I always felt that I knew what she needed. She could just look at me, and I knew what to do. I loved watching Alina interact with her, and she wore motherhood well, even if she recoiled at the thought. Alina's voice would change when talking to her. The cadence would slow, and she spoke clearly. She was stern yet forgiving and was unafraid to reprimand if need be. She will be a great mother someday if she's not already.

We walked home from the hospital, and the air had the Land's sting of midwinter. We walked the sidewalk, and Anya did her best to avoid stepping on any of the cracks presenting themselves in front of her. Alina and I each held one of her tiny palms; gripping tightly, we swung her into the air. We felt like a family, and I truly wished we were.

The content I felt with them subsided as soon as Alina and I were alone together. With buffers, we were better, ideal, and whole, but without them, we were calamitous, a shipwreck, slowly succumbing to the rapidity of rogue waves and the pounding of rain. The long circling and persistent spiraling eventually gave way, and soon enough, even in the company of Anya, Alina and I seemed to idle. There was a constant downtrend seen in the books of a bankrupt business. The unending, nerve-racking insecurity forced me further down a hole. In hindsight, now I see that I have myself to blame, as one can only control his action and the ways in which he responds to difficult situations. As was then and still is today, my reactions to things out of my control are of the self-destructive type. Even after going back and coming back, little was seen in the way of change.

MISERY IN OCEANSIDE

Eight Months After Leaving Alina and the Land

Too far north to ever be warm, the sun sets nicely beyond the waterline. The air is always cold, and there is constant dew that rests on both the natural and man-made. Oregon's seagulls caw and other winged fowl flutter about in what seem like confused patterns. Being as I am unable to fly, confined to land-based movement, I ponder what the birds think of me, if they think of me at all. Are they remorseful toward my relative lack of freedom? Seemingly unrestricted by gravity, they flow with the wind, determining flight patterns based on air currents and temperature. I make my moves guided by emotion and the grinding pressures that only exist inside my mind. I am jealous of the bird-brained young saplings that are born with the instinct to fly. I have spent the last decade in a befuddled daze only to emerge from it with regret and contempt for myself and the ever-present desire to stay inside the daze.

I've rented a hill-side cabin overlooking the ocean. A magnificent structure, one crafted entirely in tune with nature and constructed solely of cedar. A beautiful achievement in melding nature and the mind. The result of a single vision, a vision labored and achieved. A complex of sorts, the only thing out of place is the occupant. Through its appearance, all its parts serve a purpose, with nothing misplaced and nothing superfluous. A staircase wraps in a spiral shape, running the entirety of the cabin, connecting the floors, and serving as its spine.

A place most unfit for the likes of me, I require no more than a closet and am deserved of even less. The thought has crossed my mind more times than once. *Why am I here? Why have I chosen such a beautiful backdrop for such a miserable existence?* Granted, I was on somewhat of a high note prior to arriving. I had twelve days off the stuff before my most expected relapse. Alone, here I sit, reveling in misery of my own creation, straddling a screw-top bottle of Jim Beam, openly excoriating myself against a sunlit sky containing not a single cloud and bursting with the brightest of blues. Like a trigger primed to fire, I go down in the depths of my mind, racing in intense contemplation of the particulars. The rift that distance creates, the countless miles and changes in time zone that severs connection and facilitates a void surely to be filled by something. Alina lives peacefully now, traveling to California, which she has long desired to see. Our simultaneous decision to see the ocean now rips at my brain, scratching and tearing against the membrane, forcing its way in, no matter how long I struggle to keep it out. I give in to the only medicine I've ever known to stop the hurt, to stop the incessant clawing and lashings I rain down upon myself. Except now, I suspect, it has lost its touch, as I am left with no reprieve, nothing to dress the wounds I have incurred.

The cabin is warmed by a wood-fired stove with logs left by the owner. I strip pieces off for kindling, and the fire grows from a small flame to a raging blaze. I've spent the first of four nights, and as the duration of my stay is only just beginning, I have the urge to abandon it. As my outlook increases in bleakness, a Ponderosa pine drops needles, quietly collecting on the deck. How long before one needle falls into the pile and the support beams give way to collapsing the structure? How much more can it take?

The bones of the cabin are showing, trusses designed to please the esthetic and provide support for brutal weather. Both secure and captivating, both safe and fascinating. I stumble down the spiral staircase, crashing into bed. *Why have I come here? What was the point?* I seem to have lost it now. I felt free to test the limits of what I know can break me, and by now, I know it has.

The booze seeps in my bloodstream. Rarely do I venture into town, as I wish to remain unseen. Residing in my cabin, glued to the bottle, I count the minutes until departure. Quite possibly, this whole excursion is a dream or, more fitting, a nightmare, one from which I will soon awake. She will be there next to me as she always was. A lesson in degeneration, a study of suffering, a long list of mistakes I can't take back. Forcing myself to recall them, I replay them over and over in the theater of my mind. There is no intermission nor any second screening. A picture on continuous loop plays scenes of regret and misgivings. I am the main character. The protagonist and antagonist, both roles custom-made, fit like a second skin. I am alone here, and that is how I prefer it. I have made up my mind that I prefer solitude, as there exists little to sabotage. Nothing to ruin except my own standing and this sick, twisted pleasure of grief and undying remorse.

There are trails here, in the hills and cliffs that follow along the beaches. I settle on one for the fresh air and an attempt to quiet my mind. I traverse these trails beaten down from repeated use. I look toward the finish before I have begun. I'd rather it all be over because at least then there is a conclusion. The clean air of the ocean smells strange as I was once accustomed to poor air quality and brake dust.

She escaped her smog-filled atmosphere, trading traffic for Big Sur. Leaving behind the mundane, her extemporaneous inclinations provide her the freedom she so desires and projects a sense of spontaneity, something I will always love her for. Twenty years ago, I would have had no idea. Today, life is mostly online, and I am made aware even when I care not to look, even when I care not to know. Like a dagger driven through my eyes, I see her out West. Through a telephone, I see a ten-second short glimpse into her life. I don't have to look, but for some reason, I feel I do, almost like a nervous habit, like eating your fingernails or picking your skin. I can't escape it. How I despise modern technology. All the things that are meant to connect us just rip us apart, shrink our brains, and feed into our lesser qualities. All its gifts, the sum of human knowledge, yet I use it for the most immoral of means. Tossing my phone into the vast expanse of the ocean never sounded better, but I clutch it, holding on ever tighter as if want and need are the same. I envisioned long walks on the beach lit by the moon, but now I smoke cigarettes on the deck, laughing in the face of despair, drunk beyond coherence. Swaying, hoping that my weight added to the pile of needles collected in the corner pushes us past the weight limit and plunges us into darkness. I have no regard for the needles, as nature has no regard for me.

Conversations on our couch now bounce inside my brain. I heard her, but I did not have the ability to bring her wants and my own into coexistence. It was like I was being torn apart, limb from limb, my mind melting in attempts to preserve whatever remained of us in those final days. She had no idea of the war raging inside of me, no inkling of the poison I was ingesting every day. I was selfishly lashing out when she attempted to steer me in a straight line. I was drowning, thrown from the clarity of a sober mind and clean soul.

I use all the might I can muster to turn back the hands of time, begging Father Time to allow me reclamation of moments long passed. Nothing can be altered, as the events are set in stone. Frustrations agonizing, battles lost, and sieges laid.

From the beginning, I was already gone. Strung out, holding it together as best I could. How pathetic I must have been in her eyes. I was once lost in them but later became lost in the demands of coke and pills. I am to blame for my actions. I cannot permit myself to scapegoat genetics or predisposition to drugs, as I do not believe that I had no choice. I made a conscious choice to abuse them, suffering the consequences. I relinquished what was taken. I developed a chemical dependence that was part of my construction. I bear the responsibility; I am to blame. That person I was is *me*; he is in there, caged like an animal, cut off from the light of day. I gave up what I valued most for a high and false impression of self-confidence. In the wreckage of my former self, I am there, pleading for change, pleading to recognize what I am losing.

My chance forsaken, I must pay the toll to travel this road, to conceptualize the full size and scope of the loss, to bathe in the regret I feel every moment of every day. The jumbled memories cataloged inside my brain are slowly fading, losing them somewhere between gratefulness and regret.

Now, I stay somewhat broken, discombobulated, and out of whack, my internal mechanisms running afoul and at half capacity. I walk the earth jilted by my own hand. How I long to travel back in time to redress and reprise our time together. To be in the land I love with the woman I love. I falter now; my engines fail to fire. I gather what I can and muster an effort, still moving with a pin in my side and an itch I can't scratch—a wound that just won't heal. I tried to cast her out, sever correspondence, and denounce her existence, but I'm left with the memory, with the essence of her touch still lingering on my body, her breath in my ear, warming my insides. Thrashing about, I sweat her out like a fever that has not yet run its course. I'm left half human, half open, and strewn about, lost in this world, living in another.

She never noticed when I was fucked up. I could eat Adderall and run lines in our bathroom, and she never suspected a thing. I drank about a pint of whiskey a night and stayed up until 4:00 a.m. regularly. The effects of Adderall and cocaine mixed with alcohol are not the most conducive chemicals to slumber. I would sit on the couch and wait for the wave of anxiety to wash over me, when I started to notice the sun peaking up. I awoke most afternoons surprised to be alive, our home still somewhat in order. After acknowledging my existence, I checked below where the couch cushions meet, feeling for an empty pint of Jim Beam. Sometimes, I dumped the empties behind the couch, and I would surely have to grab those before she stumbled upon them. The bottles in the couch would need to be removed, as she liked to rotate the cushions frequently. She smoked hookah constantly and needed a quaint environment. She was a woman who created her own element; she was a natural nester. Another stash spot was the inside of my coat pocket, but she busted me one day, so I had to move it to a spot behind the fridge, where she couldn't see, even when standing on her tiptoes.

During that time, I was flying above the clouds and frying my brain. I stayed steadfast in my allegiance to drugs. Rotting out in front of her eyes, not reaching out for help, I continued to slowly commit suicide. Depending on the amount of drugs, I couldn't get hard, but she was rarely interested, and neither was I.

I remember, while on a trip in the Dominican Republic, we were walking after dark, the sand pressing through our toes, the moon reflecting off the water. There were beach chairs neatly placed and all in a row. I could see the light in her eyes, highlighting her more pronounced features. I blurted out, "I will marry you." She laughed as she always did when I said exactly what was on my mind. Generally, speaking my mind includes some tongue-in-cheek, but in that moment, I meant it, and a part of me still does.

Of all the trips we embarked on together, that trip to DR was my favorite because it felt like a genuine vacation. We were skirting the headwinds of the Land in midwinter and escaping the crippling defeat developing slowly in our apartment. The trip was her parents' idea, and we gladly obliged, as I have immense respect for her mother, and while I had yet to meet her father, that is where I would. I was drunk and, as usual, missed the opportunity to ask him for her hand. The fog that was my head seems so distant when I look back, so completely foreign, yet that person is exactly me.

Her mother is an incredible human being, elegant, indestructible, seemingly born with class, and truly sophisticated. Born in the Soviet Union, she knows strife and struggle. She told amazing stories like none I've heard before. They should be written. It was a pleasure to even catch her gaze. To converse with her was both visceral and cerebral, as she is as intelligent as she is beautiful. She is unstoppably graceful and stern of constitution. It was truly a pleasure to know her. She has a very smooth style, one rarely seen today. Both youthful and wise, she was tactful in speech. She once provided me with advice, and it was advice I should have taken. I failed to listen and neglected to incorporate it. I miss her and her Russian accent greatly, all the FaceTime calls with her daughter and the way Alina's voice would mimic the high pitch of a child's when speaking to her. I miss the *chka*—her mother would add to her name, never understanding what it meant until I asked and read more Dostoevsky.

In a way, I relished their many similarities and very much looked forward to Alina at an older age, taking on the traits I saw in her mother. There was, however, an elephant in the room. Neither of them knew of it; I hid it well and indulged like a gluttonous Roman. I was taking all her natural gifts for granted, as if she would always be there and I could get by without trying. She knew her worth, and I knew it, too, yet I failed to pay the price. I pay a price now, however, one I do not have enough to cover, one where I'm stretched so thin that I fear I will drive myself either mad or sick, both of which I deserve and both of which I am careening toward. Her image still flashes in my mind, still crashing like lightning and shaking like thunder.

It would appear to me that, after these four nights are done and I make my way inland, these feelings won't subside. Maybe that's the difficulty in experiencing something as profound as love and as shattering as losing it. I wanted to stay decrepit inside and ignore her callings of a broken heart. If I would have listened, where would she be today? With me? Maybe. Who's to know? But at least I would have presented my true feelings, held not under soil and dirt, flowering, blooming, casting shadows over what she required. When insisting on misaligned priorities, I overlooked our good moments, enduring a blindness and a coldness that would only get worse with time. Loathing one's reflection, the problem stares back. There is nothing to blame, nowhere to lay fault, save at my feet. There is misery in Oceanside; there is misery in me.

LOVING & LEAVING

Alina glided down Milwaukee Ave, floating an inch above cracked pavement. She was a notch above everyone around her. Too good for The Land, yet she fit perfectly inside it. Without effort, she was subtly graceful, the hard lines of her frame cut out against time. The tribulations she faced at an early age gave her an edge so smooth yet so cutting. She was intimidating while entirely approachable. Her mind a maze, unchartered, with no map in existence, the route had to be burned in the brain. One must embark to know her; one must journey to reach her corners. She was as deep as the ocean and as unknown at her deepest part. She was made for the sun, made for the warmth that raptures the body. An anomalous being, a needle in the haystack of ordinary humanity. I knew, like Icarus, I was in for a fall, but the temptation forced me. I had to enter her mind. Noise ceased around her; she was calming yet aroused my greatest energy. Indescribable and unfathomably special, to say the least. She wore a red beret with a leather jacket, tight blue jeans, and Doc Marten boots, rocking little to no makeup, her dirty blond, wavy hair, a couple thin rings, and a golden necklace with the letter F on it. Any day with her was the best day I could conjure. Seldom does man have the chance to witness the likes of her, and even rarer is to be on the receiving end of her affections.

She was a Russian doll, both literally and figuratively. She had many layers, and the center was the smallest. She was guarded yet free; she was open yet walled. All people have multiple sides and varying degrees of personality, but she was different, difficult to read, and more stubborn than most. Cold to the touch yet warm when she wanted. She showed no consistent emotion and had little regard for the softer sensibilities of others. She was brash and a real challenge to argue with, as she was always sharp in disagreements and well informed in her grievances. I always thought she would have made a great lawyer, but that would require thoughtfulness and the desire to get out of her own way. She was not to be imposed upon and had little patience for anything she couldn't understand. Her lack of understanding extended to the feelings of others. She would complain about the impositions others heaved onto her—bosses, coworkers, neighbors, strangers, me, or her family. She granted no room to feel; she saw the world and had no time to imagine your vision. I envision, if her heart carries her to a long life, she will be one of those crotchety old women, sweeping their front porch step, angrily shooing away children and kind passersby.

After we moved in together, our relationship soured. She became distant and indifferent. I could feel her beginning to despise me. I was a ship lost at sea; I had no direction to follow. I attempted to make her happy, but the more I tried, the more unhappy she became. Like a switch had been flipped, she was suddenly not the person I knew. She was withdrawn and disliked almost everything I said or did. I wasn't exactly sure as to why. In fact, I remember thinking that she was unhappy— that much was clear. As to why, that confounded me.

I was a leech, a bottom-feeder living off the crumbs of her love. Few and far between, she dropped them for me to gather up and gorge on. I was withering, dying on the vine, begging to be plucked, consumed, or discarded, outcomes that forced a conclusion, but I never received one. I was barely even a person in those days, hardly alive and approaching death—death of the mind and body, as my soul was long gone. It would take more than her love to revive it.

We spent two years in Bucktown. One year of fighting, the other making up. We were like oil and water, cats and dogs, wine, and whiskey. I often think about how our outcome could have been different. Many moments are spent deep in contemplation, all solutions forgone as our time is long past. There are many words I wish to take back.

I'm unsure what started first—the drugs or the abuse. I met my cocaine dealer, Lito, at the bar next door to our apartment. Alina and I had had one of our famous blowout fights at some bar in Wicker Park and took separate rides home. I arrived before her and decided to stop into Gallery Cabaret for a double shot of Jim before returning home and continuing our hostile argument. I approached the bar and ordered my usual, which the barkeep was reluctant to pour, as he could tell I was in a fit and already past inebriation. I slammed the highball down and peered around the room. Gallery attracted an interesting crowd, as each night of the week was a different theme and a different base. One night was open mic for comedy, another was an open mic for bands, and another was an urban hip-hop night. Saturdays tended to be the liveliest, as the Land is a city for drinkers, and bars are the place to be for the more social of alcoholics.

I approached a man, maybe five feet, nine inches tall, and struck up a conversation.

"You know where I can get some coke?"

"Shit, I can sell you some."

"That was easy," I said, smiling, drunk and internally desperate to feel something other than strife.

"One sec," he said, obviously pleased that a new customer had found him.

"I need to run out to my car and grab it real quick. Fifty for a half G, and one hundred for a whole."

I elected to go with a half gram, as one can be most unsure of quality when purchasing cocaine from a stranger in a dark dive bar. I proceeded to the ATM, withdrawing sixty dollars in increments of twenty, and broke one of them on a Pabst Blue Ribbon beer. By the time I had taken my first drink, he was back and ready to make the deal. Lito was comfortable at Gallery. I would later come to find that he was a regular and was on good terms with all two of the staff members and almost all the patrons. I handed him the fifty dollars, and he put the small bag of cocaine in my shirt pocket. The bag was the corner of a small plastic sandwich bag, the open part tied into a knot to secure the powder.

"Here you go, brotha," he said. "Take my number down. I deliver, and it's good shit."

"Thanks, yeah, let me get that," I said, pleased to have a new contact.

I walked into the bathroom—a small, cramped room, rarely cleaned. A place to piss and shit and seldom wash your hands. There was one stall and one urinal in the corner, filthy from overuse. I entered the stall and poured out a small amount of blow on the back of the toilet tank. I used my credit card to crush the small rocks and a rolled-up dollar bill as a straw. I bent down to snort the line, immediately feeling that familiar sting in my right nostril. I jerked my head upward and, closing my left nostril with my finger, breathed in deeply with the right.

Make sure to get it all in there, I thought to myself.

I closed off the bag, making sure to keep the contents intact, unrolled my dollar, placed it back in my wallet, and wiped any remaining residue off the toilet with my finger, rubbing it along my gumline. The stuff was decent; he would have a returning customer and a faithful one at that. I stuck around the bar, chatting with him for maybe twenty minutes and two more trips to the bathroom; I think I pissed once. I crossed the street and met my front door, opening it and walking up the stairs. I lifted my foot slowly to each stair, reluctant to enter the apartment. There was a monster waiting for me, ready to fight, with a gut full of booze.

"Where the fuck were you? You left before I did. What took so long?"

"I stopped into Gallery for another drink. I really don't

want to fight with you," I said, fully aware of what she would say next.

"Oh, you don't want to fight. Because you're a bitch, half a man?"

"Yeah, Alina, I'm a bitch, half a man," I said, sarcastically, entering the bathroom.

This initial entrance into the bathroom would be the first of many trips where she thought I was freshening up or pissing, but it was to crush cocaine on the back of our toilet tank. That night was like many to come, first an eagerness to argue, and then an escalation to physical violence—like clockwork. I could count on the stages of her anger. Upon exiting our bathroom, I was met with blows, one striking the side of my head and the others meeting my torso. I staggered back into the bathroom shouting, "Oh, shit," or some other expletive.

The next morning, all was well in our household. The birds outside were chirping, and frost was collecting on the window. I was hungover as all hell, and so was she. We didn't speak about the events from the night before, carrying on with our day like it never happened. We ate breakfast together, and there was an obvious tension neither one of us dared to mention, acting as though the prior evening was a one-off. I thought that her acknowledgment would bring it into reality, and I was okay with leaving it in last night. I imagine we then took our dog to the dog park or went for a walk around our neighborhood, smoking cigarettes and looking into other people's homes, half wishing we could trade lives with them.

We carried on like this for a year or so, drinking at night, fighting, and spitting fire. I began to believe she genuinely enjoyed our spats. I became a punching bag. I was a drunk but a peaceful one at that. I never struck her or even placed a finger on her. I had drugs to ease my temper.

One night, she was mad and red all over, a flaring flame in each eye. I was high, as usual, and drunk like a sailor. We both imbibed a fifth of Jim Beam mixed with hot water and waited for the fireworks. Fists began flying toward the end of the night, with shouting already in full swing. Blows reigned down in our kitchen and followed me around our apartment. I remember wanting her to stop. I just wanted to get away from her, but I had nowhere to go except the cold wooden planks of a park bench down the street. I would often take refuge there if she allowed me to escape the apartment. Mostly, I would cower into a corner and cover up, using anything as a barrier between us to create distance, making her strikes easier to evade, a bob and weave, so to speak. I remember, on this night, we were in the kitchen, and I used our recycle bin to create space, but she used the metal lid, jabbing it into my abdomen, lurching me over, and punching down against the back of my head. I tried to cover up, but she had me, and she knew it. She kicked my hip, pushing me to the ground, and poured what was left of our whiskey on my heaped body. I was nothing to her.

Her words were as cutting as her knuckles, as there was nothing she wouldn't say. There existed no line between decency and disrespect. She would fly off the handle and berate me, but the longer this carried on, the less I heard any of it. To me, it was obvious she was dealing with something in her own mind that came out in the form of aggression.

She had this ear-piercing shriek like that of a bat.

"You aren't shit compared to your friends. You're embarrassed that they're so much further ahead than you."

I still have a scar above my left eye, where she hit me with a glass cup, shattering it against my temple. If I didn't have my guard up, she would punch me square in the face, popping my nose like a crushed grape, blood spewing. To keep it from splattering on the floor, I pooled blood in my hand, running to a sink. She was crazed and entirely cold, and no words could be said to calm her rage. Chasing me through our second-floor walkup, she was alive with blind hatred. She pounded on doors I found refuge behind, knowing it was only a matter of time before I had to come out. After throwing my clothing in our garden and dumping the contents of my wallet in the street below, I would humiliatingly pick them up. Other times, I was forced to collect my belongings that she threw down the hallway, down the stairs, and out the door. At least six times, I had to retrieve my wardrobe.

"Bitch" was her favorite insult, as she would say it with such a cadence, it made my skin crawl. She truly meant it when she said it. I could tell by the force she used, pushing air through her windpipe.

She came at me with a kitchen knife saying, "I'll fucking kill you. Just leave the apartment."

I left.

I walked to Holstein Park down Oakley Avenue and tried to sleep on a park bench. I chose a spot with tree coverage, trying to avoid streetlamps and police. I saw the woman who lives on Western & McLean, hunched over and passed out on a nearby bench. There was a forty-ounce beer inside a paper bag laying on its side next to her. I wanted to talk to her; she had a soul. I was desperate to share what I was experiencing, but she looked peaceful. I let her sleep. I laid there for several hours in the dead of winter, struggling to keep warm, but if she could do it, so could I. The sun was beginning to rise as the sky began to take on a bright hue, leaving behind the pitch-black of night. I figured she had to be long asleep by then, so I made my way home.

Before running out several hours prior, I managed to grab my keys, which, times before, I seldom could. I entered our warmed apartment and slumped on the couch with my clothes on. A few moments later, I heard rustling in the bedroom and knew I must have woken her. I heard a drawer open and its contents being dumped out. Something was about to happen. I opened my eyes. Immediately, I felt a dull pain at the top of my head and heard a crash against the wall. I kept a small combination lock in that drawer; I suddenly saw it on the floor below me.

I felt my head, and my hair was wet. It hadn't snowed, so I knew it was blood. I was at the end of my rope right then and hoping for another. I was impartial to what she chose to do next. She could have killed me or left me there, and either way, I was fine with it. I was sick of doing drugs every day just to feel something, and I was sick of her nightly violence. I just wanted to sleep, as I had been up for almost forty-eight hours, high and flying the night before.

In the half-light, she was standing by the bedroom door, shouting, "I told you to leave."

I couldn't tell her about my drug use, afraid of how she would react. I was a junkie with no friends, unless you count the questionable relationships with my dealers.

Death is a funny thing to desire; it goes against all human biology and evolution. I wasn't even human in those days, though, moving only mechanically alone and feeding a fire. I remember hoping and wishing for one soul, one soul even as filthy as the woman on Western & McLean.

My inevitable decline continued as I quit my job at a raman restaurant to get high day after day. I would leave our apartment around 9:00 a.m. and stay out until about 5:00 p.m. I spent hours in the Bucktown-Wicker Park Branch library researching articles about something called the coronavirus ravishing China. High out of my mind and picking at my fingernails, I smoked cigarettes out front and hoped Alina wouldn't pass by and catch me in another one of my lies. I experienced a touch of psychosis, and it showed when I returned to our apartment. Something about this respiratory illness pointed toward societal collapse, and I knew it would eventually make its way across the ocean and begin to spread infection, invading the consciousness of politicians, businesses, and the citizenry. I pleaded with Alina to trust me and follow my lead, but she thought I was crazy, and I undoubtedly was, but I got one thing right. Life as we knew it would change drastically, and our world would constrict further and turn in on itself. A few weeks later, north and south switched, and a tidal wave was off in the distance—a tidal wave no one could ignore as the media began to pump the pandemic through its airwaves, and it eventually crashed against everyone breathing and against those who thought they would continue breathing for only a short while longer. Panic, panic in the grocery stores as people scurried like ants to hunker down in quickly planned preparation. Anxiety at a level I've never seen, and fear on faces as if it were painted on with a metallic spray paint so vibrant and clear, shining against the fluorescent lights of Jewel-Osco. Nobody was cutting coupons or bargain shopping—they were grabbing at anything that remained on the shelves. Toilet paper received a great deal of attention, but most everything else was either out of stock or inside peoples' shopping carts. I tried to remain calm, as I felt like a million bucks. After all, I had drugs in my pocket, and there was a twisted feeling of righteousness inside my chest, considering that I saw this coming from however many miles it would take to walk to China.

The collective response to the glorified flu shut us in for the final six months of our time together. Alina and I had decided that, to preserve our sanity and my safety, we would end our relationship and become friends as best as we could. We maintained our lease and lived together but separate. I would sleep on the couch most nights or in bed with her when she was feeling lonely. Our lease was up in September, and we spent our March birthdays thinking the world was going to end. The Land that I fell in love with four years prior sat idle, almost frozen in time. The lights that were always on were now shut off, leaving the ice-glittered streets to be darkened and vacant. The girl I fell in love with three years prior now sat alone on our couch, buried in anxiety, nervous about the future, scared for her family. I took no joy in seeing her like that; in fact, I hated it. She was a flower, wilted and worried the sun would never shine again. I played the role of jester to uplift her spirits, but everyone during that time was stuck inside their head, wheels spinning and going nowhere.

This was the worst-case scenario to befall. I now had free time and free money to use, receding deeper, deeper into the abyss. The hatred she had for me morphed into a desperate friendship, as I was all she had, and I had drugs. I cared not to preserve myself; I cared to be high and watch the time pass. The idea of us parting ways seemed unrealistic and was not even a concept I considered. I was set in one mode, my engines revved, pistons firing. I was wildly out of control. I started my day with 40 mg of Adderall, followed by bong hits to calm the clenching. I polished off whatever Jim Beam was still in our kitchen, making plans to buy more. After avoiding lunch, I popped another 60 mg and walked the dog. By the late afternoon, I wore a face full of powder, dumping whiskey down my throat. After sundown, I was on coke bag number two with a sweaty forehead and a pep in my step. If I bought a fifth earlier in the day, that was getting near empty, so I would need at least a pint more. About midnight, Alina would go to bed, and I would pound whiskey, peering from our living room window, searching for constellations.

Death was all around us, closing in, it's aim set on the living. It was the end of so much, and a beginning seemed a long way off. I suppose beginnings are as inevitable as endings, but the latter surely feels longer, as the snuffing of life is a process, and life happens in an instant. Eventually, Alina and I parted. Early September, when the trees began to prepare for winter. We embraced for the last time on our sidewalk facing McLean, and as quickly as she came into my life, she was suddenly entirely out of it. In hindsight, there should have been some grand gesture, where I chase after her and tell her that I don't want to leave her and explain how we can work on it and live happily ever after, mimicking scenes from famous movies, but instead, I entered the rented Kia Sorento, packed with what was left of my life in the Land, and set off for southeastern Washington.

Through the buttes and mesas of Wisconsin, I watched an

eagle control the sky. In the prairies and endless farmland of South Dakota, I navigated open space of a country I had yet to see. The wilderness and high plains of Wyoming gave me room to breathe. Through the river valleys and badlands of Montana, I laid bare the impossible past. Running long stretches of empty highway and moving through the mountains of Idaho, I finally arrived at the base of the Blues.

Life is a continual process of learning. Experiences recalled at varying intervals reveal different lessons and serve as reminders. If there is any takeaway from the past five years, it is certainly that some things lost can never be regained, no matter the level of effort to retrieve them. When loving is lost, leaving is the only thing to do.

EPILOGUE

Entering Paddington's open-air station, my hat catches a gust and blows up behind me. I give chase for thirty feet before I catch up, but now, I've got ten before the street. The pack I've shouldered for the last three weeks begins to tip, the weight on my back shifting from side to side. I know I'm going down without more runway. My possessions are shaken from their pockets. People begin to notice, shouting as I blow past them, headed straight for the curb. I save a crash-landing a foot from the pavement. I collect my scattered inventory, do a bow, and proceed to the Heathrow Express. My time was up in London Town, but I didn't want to leave.

CPSIA information can be obtained
at www.ICGtesting.com
Printed in the USA
BVHW041448190523
664344BV00004B/25